I Am a Woman of

G.R.I.T.

By

BEATRICE MOORE

Printed in the United States of America

ISBN 978-0-9990422-6-7

Sole Surrender Publishing

Contact Email: abluchin@sbcglobal.net

Dedication

I am a woman of GRIT- Grace, Restoration, Integrity, and Transformation. Let this be my legacy that I leave for my children, Macy, DJ, and Curtis.

To those giants:

> Many of whom I will never know the names of, on whose shoulders I stand, so I would not have to pick cotton, sit in the back of the bus and not be able to live my dreams, and

To my family:

> My grandfather, Reverend Jesus Garcia, who was the first man to show me love. Norris and Helen, my parents, who did not live to see my transformation and;

> My darling sister Bertha who was taken too soon, but whose spirit of determination and fight I carry within me;

> My Aunt Verlene, who gave me the love of education,

And for my husband, who helped me to understand how to give even when it hurts,

I thank you.

Table of Contents

Preface

Hey there! As I prayed over how to write this book, I called on God to lead me. I know now that He wanted me to write this book in an intimate style meant to reflect our casual conversations. These casual conversations breathed new life into me and allowed me to develop an authentic and meaningful relationship with Him. I know you have been hand-picked to receive this message because He led you to it. You are my sister in Christ, and through this book, I pray that God will allow us to become forever connected. As you read, I pray that you build your wisdom and confidence as your relationship with God flourishes. As you read, you will get a glimpse into my window of life and experience how I had to seek God's wisdom and direction. My goal is to impart to you the lessons I learned and perhaps rescue some of you in advance from being in that unenviable position of wishing you had taken a moment to simmer down before you did that thing you did and now regret doing it! One of my biggest lessons was to allow God to be that confidant when I needed someone to act as a sounding board – yes, let Him be there for you. As you immerse yourself in this book, I pray that you accept it as a living breathing gift from the Highest God!

I want you to be ultimately transformed by the end of this book – make that your goal as you begin to read. Jesus is walking with you right now. I asked him to guide my thoughts and pour into me a message of healing—healing in the areas of faith, family, relationships, finance, and your future.

Grit means tenacity, and to make it, you must hang in there! If you want your faith to reach its full potential, there will be storms to test it! So, get ready! You want your family and relationships strong; get ready to experience the weight and the wait that it takes to build spiritual muscle to make it. You desire financial increase, so you can be the lender and not the borrower; get ready to give more than your fair share. Your future needs direction or a shot of energy, and you just want to know if you're in the right place, then get ready to learn how to listen with spiritual ears for God's soft, small voice.

I don't know about you, but I made a conscious decision that I would not wander in the wilderness for 40 years (or 40 months for that matter) on an 11-day journey because of a lack of faith and obedience. I just don't have that kind of time to waste.

Speak to this reader now, my precious Lord. Begin to narrate the images, and download Your will into the reader. My dearest reader, you are on a supernatural journey that requires supernatural faith. Don't try to explain anything to anyone. They most likely aren't ready to receive it anyway and may try to rationalize a way out for you. So, shut off the outside voices, and hear from the Master who loves you because you're His masterpiece, and He wants to give you the Master's perfect peace! Do not allow a seat at your table for the enemy who doesn't want you to pray. He wants to distract you, whisper things into your ear that negate what God has promised you, and he often uses those who are close to you to do so.

Oh, stop right there! Take that in. What peace are you seeking? Ask Him for it right now—yes, right now. Don't delay. Just start speaking to him now. It is time to develop a relationship with God. Don't be afraid to ask God for the big dreams that are planted inside you.

Holy Father, I need peace in the following areas of my life:

_____

_____

_____

_____

_____

I lean on your word, Psalm 29:11, *"The LORD gives strength to his people; the LORD blesses his people with peace."* Because I am your child, I know that You will bless me with Your promise of strength and perfect peace! The peace I seek is that which comes from You, God. It surpasses my understanding, and it will allow me to hope, provide me with strength, and enable me to live with joy! I serve a gracious God of peace, and You promised to take care of me, comfort me, provide for me, and restore my hope and joy! I want to experience Your perfect peace, and I am trusting You and allowing You to work out Your plans for my life. No matter what circumstances I face now or in the future, I confidently rest assured that You, my God, are working all things together for my good and Your glory! I trust and obey Your omniscient power and glory, in Jesus' name, Amen.

PURPOSE

I am a woman of GRIT— Grace, Restoration, Integrity, and Transformation!

I don't know why God chose me, but He did, and I was obedient to His call on my life. When He knocked, I answered. When He commanded, I obeyed. Then all hell broke loose in my life, but I cannot say that it was not expected. You see, the enemy does not want ministry assignments fulfilled. Satan wants nothing more than to see the church die on the vine. He has spent centuries wreaking havoc on men and women of God to stop the spread of God's word. Not only that, he wants marriages to fail, and families to rot like fallen fruit that went unharvested. The stench of rotting fruit filling the air is the ultimate fragrance to Satan because that rotting fruit represents lives unfulfilled, destinies denied, and lives unlived.

Spoiler alert! This is not a book in which I share every titillating detail of the ups and downs and the ins and outs of my marriage. I'd rather focus on the lessons I learned as I walked through the valley of the shadow of the death of my marriage with God walking beside me. I also recognized that the enemy was also walking with me, but I placed God in a position of authority and leadership as I walked. I did not give up or in. I followed God's Positioning Signal, which was far superior to my own GPS.

My valley experience was used to strengthen me in a way I would never have been strengthened if I had been allowed to remain in my position of comfort and security. The disruption came. I was plucked up like a seedling and my roots broken and bruised. I was transplanted into an abandoned landscape where there was no sunshine, no rain, no life, just desolation – or so I thought. You see, at the onset of the disruption, I held a pity party and never looked up. I just kept looking down, distraught over what I had lost, and where I now found myself. I was overlooking the small miracles each day that God was placing at my feet as I walked through the valley. Can anyone relate to this? My problem was that I wasn't looking up. I was so caught up in my personal grief that I was totally missing God's perfect plan for my life. I wonder how many people have done the same thing. I was paralyzed for many days, not knowing which way to turn or move. My life as I knew it had been washed away like a house during a Category 5 hurricane.

I settled into an unhealthy, unproductive rhythm of replaying what went wrong, and what was and wasn't said. I also had sleepless nights filled with coulda's, woulda's, and shoulda's! Can I get an "Amen" here from somebody?

Then, one day, God was calling my name, and I had the audacity to look up. And when I did, everything changed! You see, looking down, all I saw was dirt—you know, dark dirt. Looking up, there was sunshine and sky. I realized that day that God had made me a woman of GRIT - Grace, Restoration, Integrity, and Transformation. Now, when I looked down, the ground wasn't so dark because I allowed the light of God to shine on, in, and through me. I saw through new eyes, and my tiny miracles I had inadvertently stepped over now came into focus. You know, the miracle that I was still in my right mind; I still had a roof over my head; I still had my children, and they were safe and healthy! God had my back. I want to share with you my story, or should I say the story of how God used my darkest hours to create my brightest days through His amazing grace, the restoration of my soul, the rebuilding of integrity, and the beautiful transformation of my heart.

I didn't want to keep this lesson of GRIT to myself, and God didn't intend for me to be selfish with this gift of GRIT. So, the purpose of my pain was to unlock a passion for God that was already hibernating inside me. I had to be uprooted and replanted. My potential is being realized with the writing of this book. I am so grateful that God loved me enough not to be satisfied with the mediocre life I was living.

> 2 Corinthians 12:8-9 states, *"Three times I pleaded with the Lord about this, that it should leave me. But he said to me, 'My grace is sufficient for you, for my power is made perfect in weakness.' Therefore, I will boast all the more gladly of my weaknesses, so that the power of Christ may rest upon me."*

CHAPTER 1

My Encounter with Grace

Grace is the love and mercy given to us by God because God desires us to have it! Yes, God wants us to live an abundant life and have it all. Who doesn't want it all? The funny thing about grace is that it is not given to us because of anything we have done to earn it. It is not a created substance of any kind. Grace, simply put is a favor, the free and undeserved help that God gives us to respond to His call to become children of God – his daughters, partakers of the divine nature and of eternal life. Grace is a spontaneous gift from God to you and me. God's gift of grace is generous, free, totally unexpected, and absolutely undeserved.

I can look back over my life and see so many instances of God's grace. I must be honest with you. For years I really thought I was responsible for much of my success. You know what I mean. I had secured the education, made the right moves, networked, studied, and perfected my craft. Yes, I was successful, had a great career, a loving husband, and a beautiful home – or so I thought. Out of nowhere, I had the rug of a stable life pulled from under me and had no one to lean on, but God. That is when I was finally able to reflect and see my life as a series of grace-given interventions orchestrated by God.

I found myself all alone in a huge, beautiful, and empty house with no other footsteps but my own, no other voice in the night but my own, no other heartbeat in my bed but my own, and no other touch but my own to hold me through the night. Fifteen years of marriage blew up in my face with the shutting of a door followed by the faint sound of footsteps exiting. The crank of the car was drowned out by my cries in the closet with my face to the floor. Tears created a cool resting place for my face that was flushed with the heat of hurt, pain, anger, and disbelief. Satan showed up in my household *"seeking whom he may devour."* (1 Pet. 5:8) Satan *"came to steal, kill, and destroy."* (John 10:10) Oh, I ached. I cried out. I agonized for weeks until God's grace showed up in the form of friends that He led to my doorstep to visit once I was strong enough to share through my embarrassment and feeling of failure.

Then there were the dozens of calls to me and the occasional card in the mail. Please, dear reader, never underestimate the power of a phone call or a card! I was struggling in every aspect of my shattered life that was veiled in a cloud of deception called perfection. My perfect life was exposed for what it was and what it wasn't. I became completely transparent, and this transparency was needed in order to expose me to myself so that I could experience the magnificence of a God-given, abundant grace.

God sent me His grace in the form of God-fearing and God-believing women who ministered to me nonstop. They coached me through my pain and helped me to realize that in this pain was my purpose and promise for my future. These prayer warriors were the undeserved help that God sent me. I was abandoned yet not alone. In solitude, I began to seek God more than ever. I finally established the relationship with Him that He had always deserved and desired.

I finally learned to live an abundant life during a three-month period when my bank account hovered at all-time lows for months. Added to that were the humiliation and embarrassment of debt collectors calling, and insufficient funds becoming routine. Honestly, I don't even know how I made ends meet. It was definitely a Matthew 14:13-21 miracle to meet multiple mortgage payments, car payments, summer utility bills in the heat of a Houston summer, credit cards and just day-to-day living expenses on less than $2500 for three months. I was operating from a rapidly depleting savings account. That was not working! Oh, did I mention that I am self-employed? So, there are no sick days or vacation days for me. No work means no money! Yes, during this time, I learned what abundance meant. Hard to believe, right? But that is how God works.

I gave God all my attention when Satan gained access to my marriage and stripped me of all the creature comforts that had become my idols in one way or another. Oh, do not think for one minute that in order for something to be an idol, you have to place it on an altar and burn incense to it. I realized that I had put so many people and things ahead of my worship, my prayer, my spiritual growth, and my spiritual gifts. But I was a church-going, church-working, tithing Christian woman! How dare God do this to me? My arrogance was amazingly stupid and misplaced but perfectly appropriate for someone who had failed to establish the right relationship. You see, I had a relationship but not the right relationship—you know, the one God wanted all along. Instead of reaching for God immediately, I was angry and in denial. God still provided me with the gift of grace. Oh, how I now see things clearly in the rearview mirror! I would not trade this humbling experience for all the gold in the world because what I have now is superior to gold. I have God's grace and perfect peace and joy. I am right where He wants me to be.

Now, I know three months is not a long time to suffer financially, and many people go far longer. I honestly believe that it didn't last long because I quickly got into a place of prayer, worship, and praise, and I was unrelenting with it. Church was not an option; it was a necessity. I thirsted for the Word of God and actively sought books to read and study. I also changed my television watching patterns to include more Christian-based content because my soul was hurting. When your soul is hurting, you must heal in the right place and in the right way. Prayer was happening all day long and loudly! Dancing and shouting were part of my daily praise and still are. I developed habits of prayer, praise, and worship that are here to stay.

The scripture, Philippians 4:6, *"Don't worry about anything; instead pray about everything. Tell God what you need and thank him for all he has done,"* became a constant source of strength for me. I figured out how to get through each day with prayer and supplication with thanksgiving and praise on my lips, rather than wallowing in pity and cursing God for what was now my new normal.

Grace has had and continues to have an amazing impact on my life. I now find myself intentionally extending grace to others. I think that this is part of God's divine plan for grace.

Once it is extended to us, we are bound to extend it to others, especially those who do not deserve. If we are perfectly honest, we don't deserve it either! My enemies deserve grace. My loved ones deserve grace. Strangers deserve grace. Oh my, this is where I found myself praying for those who had actively sought to destroy my marriage. I will admit it was not easy, but I mustered up the strength to do it because the voice of God whispered to me to pray for those who were against me and to speak life and light into their worlds. I whispered in response, "Really, God? Is that what I have to do?" I quickly shook that off because I knew that I needed to be obedient and immediately pray for them and to never give up. Was it easy? No! However, the more I did it, the better I felt. One day, I walked around saying, "I forgive you___" out loud, over a hundred times! To get through this, God gave me grace, and I had to develop a *"whatever it takes Lord, whatever it takes"* attitude. I did not want to miss another day of His amazing grace!

What did I learn from this that I can share with you? I learned that God wants me to share with you this simple fact: Perfect, I am NOT. I am a work in progress at the hands of the Potter who wants to create in me a new creature through Christ Jesus as discussed in 2 Corinthians 5:17.

Reflect on God's grace in your life. Where and how has it shown up? Are you needing His grace right now? If so, for what? Talk to Him right now, and thank Him for the times He has given you grace, and ask Him now to provide it when you need it. My story is no different from yours; there was conflict, loss, struggle, and redemption. Although there is a different cast of characters and circumstances, the same outcome of peace and joy through God's grace can be yours if you allow Him into your heart.

Pray with me now.

Father, we seek You in every aspect of our lives, and we thank You for Your grace that You give us because You love us. We thank You for Your unlimited supply and provision of mercy and grace, and we desire to have a heart that loves You as abundantly as You love us! We want to be filled with Your love, share that love with others, and spread Your holy name to all the corners of the earth. In Jesus' name, Amen!

Connection of Grace and Faith

A s I said earlier, I was a church-going woman and doing the church thing. I was merely going through a ritualistic process rather than establishing a relationship with the Lord. I prayed, read my Bible, and paid tithes but never had true peace until I established the relationship that caused me to thirst daily for the Lord. I had falsely interpreted what I was required to do. I fell into a trap of linking God's response to my life to my performance rather than my relationship.

Again, by definition, the word *grace* means unmerited, unearned, and undeserved favor. Remember, grace has nothing to do with you. Grace existed before you ever came to be. Another way of saying it is, "Grace is God's part." *Faith* is defined as being a positive response to what God has already provided by grace. In other words, faith is your positive response to God's grace. Faith only appropriates what God has already provided for you. Therefore, faith is your part. Grace and faith work together, and they must be in balance.

God's grace will provide for every need in your life. That provision is not performance-based. In other words, it's not based on whether you are reading the Bible enough, praying enough, going to church, or even paying your tithes. Before you ever had a financial need, God had already created the provision! Grow your faith in the soil of grace!

If you are in need of God's grace, pray now for it.

Dear Heavenly Father, I am leaning on Hebrews 4:16, where it states, *"Let us then approach God's throne of grace with confidence, so that we may receive mercy and find grace to help us in our time of need."* I approach Your throne now with confidence, and I am in need of Your grace. I acknowledge and thank You for Your grace that You have already shown when You _____

_____.

Now, I come to You asking for _____

_____,

and I have the utmost faith that You will provide.

I am praying for these people in my circle: _____

_____

_____

_____

_____.

I am grateful for _____.

Lord, I forgive_____ and I
pray for them now that they_____.

And I thank You for not only hearing my prayers but also
for the answered prayers in Jesus' name, Amen.

The Covering of Grace When Family and Relationships Are Under Attack

Trauma is real. My family, marriage, health, and finances were under attack simultaneously. Many days I felt like I had entered a wrestling ring with the devil wearing the striped referee shirt, and in each corner was an agent of the enemy who was assigned to destroy me. Imagine standing alone in the middle of what looked like a rigged match. In would jump one enemy then another, and the referee would turn away as though oblivious to what was taking place. I can see myself fighting as hard as I could. In one corner stood the enemy wearing a shirt with the names Sickness and Disease on it. I turned and looked to the next corner for relief and found another enemy holding my marriage decree in one hand and a torch the other, taunting me as he threatened to incinerate my marriage! I turned to look over my shoulder and found another one holding a money bag and throwing all the money in the air. As the bills floated aimlessly toward the floor, they turned to dust as though they never existed. The last one held pictures of my family and a pair of scissors. He laughed as he shredded the photos one by one. It was as if he was giving me a glimpse into a future without my precious children and grandchildren.

I could fight off one but not all four. They knew it, so they double-teamed me, and the referee enabled it. But God! Grace and mercy showed up and entered the ring when I called on the name of Jesus and relied on scriptures to fight for me. I had to rely on Ephesians 6:11-13: *"Put on the full armor of God so that you can take your stand against the devil's schemes. For our struggle is not against flesh and blood, but against the rulers, against the authorities, against the powers of this dark world and against the spiritual forces of evil in the heavenly realms. Therefore, put on the full armor of God, so that when the day of evil comes, you may be able to stand your ground, and after you have done everything, to stand."*

I had to learn to use the sword of the Holy Spirit to fight and put on the full armor of God! Never before had this scripture resonated with me, but in this time of trauma, all of the scriptures I had heard a thousand times began to make perfect sense.

With so much at stake, I had no choice but to believe in the Word of God because the consequences were too great, and I was surely in a battle that was greater than me! I had to learn to speak life and truth into my dead situation. Since you're reading this, I suppose you can relate to every word I'm writing to you.

I learned that in every situation, I needed to take the advice from Jeremiah 5 and know that God sees my true character, so there is no sense in trying to fake anything. I needed to make changes in me in order for my situation to change. I chose to change how I saw my pain. I also began to think about how I wanted to live in the now and stop running backward to the past that was over. I was like the women who went looking for Jesus after the crucifixion. When they sought Him in the tomb, and the angel asked them why were they seeking the living amongst the dead? God had moved on and breathed life into what was dead. I needed to move on too. God was breathing new life into me daily as I prayed, but I was missing all of that because I was wallowing in the past. I made a conscious decision to get up, get moving, and speak life into myself and every situation. I intentionally made it my plan to apply positive, life, breathing words into my daily talk with myself and others. I was tired of wrestling day and night, replaying the hurt and pain over and over, thus keeping myself on the mat of that floor in the middle of the ring with every enemy from each corner standing on my back.

I was tired of being paralyzed. I needed to breathe fresh air, but the past hurt was suffocating me until I surrendered to God and stopped trying to do this alone. Have you ever found yourself in a similar situation? You know; you were doing everything you could think of. You even tried everything friends and family suggested, but nothing changed. You began to feel the burden crushing you from the outside and exploding on the inside. That's how I felt, and that was not how I wanted my family to see me. I didn't like the negative force that was consuming me. I made a choice to live; I made a choice to give it all to God! I prayed the words from 2 Corinthians 5:17-21 over myself and asked God to *"create in me a new creature through Christ Jesus,"* and He did!

It did not happen overnight, and I still found attacks coming upon me. I was still in the ring. At one point, I found myself with a shingles outbreak that, of course, was stress-related. I nearly lost vision in one eye as a result of it, but God.

As I dealt with rejection, loneliness, and disease, I drew closer to God. At that lowest point, I cried to Him, and in the middle of that ring, the supernatural occurred. Zachariah 4:6 became an anthem in the night for me. I began to put that to work, and I humbled myself to the situation. Not by my might or power, but by His spirit was I able to rise, and the enemy was bound in each corner. I know to never get comfortable because the enemy will be back and with more vengeance. What I learned was how to fight and that God always wins! I refused to give the enemy a seat at my table, and I knew I had the power of a defiant faith planted inside me to fight.

What attacks are you under in family and relationships right now? What scriptures do you need to speak over your situation? God has a scripture for every situation. You see; He loved us so much that He anticipated every attack and made provisions for us! What a loving Father we have. Unleash your defiant faith in the face of the enemy. James 4:7 reminds us to *"submit to God; resist the devil, and he will flee!"*

I came out closer than I've ever been to God and beyond what I could ever have imagined. The scripture in Romans 8:31 states, *"What, then, shall we say in response to these things? If God is for us, who can be against us?"* This has a profound meaning that no one could explain or teach to me. I had to become an experiential student. It now speaks to my heart and is a constant whisper that I have the victory no matter what it looks like. I pray that you have this kind of faith. If not, just stay with me in this book, see my story unfold, and notice how my wings of faith grew. It is never too late, and it is never too hard for my God.

Do your work, my beloved reader. Always have scriptures ready to speak with your mouth because there will be voices to negate what God has always provided for your victory. What I learned in that battle, in that ring for months, was that my spiritual muscles were being developed to move me from being a battered patient needing the care to becoming a physician who could help others heal from their trauma.

God did not pour His grace over me in that fight so that I could get out in victory and walk away as though it never happened. He did not save me from sickness, protect my family, and provide for me financially, so I could go about my business and never share my testimony. God brought me out, and He has a requirement that I go forth and help others the same way that others helped me. He wanted to use me as a vessel to pour out upon you the same radical and defiant faith I had to develop. I learned that once I have been blessed, then I must also be a blessing. Thank you, Lord, for the multiplicative effect of your amazing grace!

My greatest blessing in all of this was the understanding that my God is greater than any enemy I will ever face. God's grace and mercy are sufficient. They are all we ever need, and we have total access to them as believers.

My legacy to my family is that I want them to see how I dealt with adversity as a woman of GRIT and a defiant woman of faith! I want them to learn from me that the enemy is not flesh and blood but of the spirit realm. People often succumb to the evil around them because they do not stay connected to God. I want my children to see that not only I'm connected, but they are as well. My children and my children's seed will be covered because I stood with God.

Right now, I'd like you to reflect on your traumatic battles, just as I have done.

- What weapons did you use to fight your battle?

- What model of a fighter were you? What legacy are you leaving? In future battles, what will be different? I want you to prepare for them because they are coming, so be intentional about how to fight.

- What did you learn from your last encounter with the enemy? Be specific. For example, what did you learn about yourself, your faith, and how to fight the enemy?

- We have relationships that extend beyond the family to include friends, neighbors, co-workers, etc. Do you see any of these people in a battle? How could you help them, and how could they help you? Have you missed opportunities to extend grace to them by offering support or prayer time?

Do you agree that there's power in praying for someone else even when you're in the midst of the battle of your life? Seek out opportunities to pray for others no matter how dire your situation looks. I found this to be wonderfully cathartic and a gift from God because it allowed me to focus my positive energy in another direction, and it fed my soul!

Let us pray together now for someone else who is going through a trial.

Father God, we come to You now, touching in agreement and asking you to watch over_____. Our sister/brother needs You in a mighty way. We know You are all-knowing and all-powerful and that You are aware of every situation _____ is facing. But we still come as sisters to stand in the gap and pray for _____ so that she/he will be able to stand the trial and come out as pure gold. Father, we pray Your promise from Isaiah 41:10 over _____. We are reminded to fear not, for You are with us. We should not be not dismayed, for You are our God. You will strengthen _____, help _____, and uphold _____ with the right hand of Your righteousness. Your grace over _____ is sufficient.

Help us to share Your gospel with _____ through words, actions, kindness, and love. Just as You have poured out Your grace on our lives, we trust You to do the same with _____. We ask this in Jesus name, and now we thank you for the wonderful works you are doing in _____'s life as we pray Holy Father. Thank you, Lord, for answering our prayers. We rejoice in the manifestation of what is already done in the heavenly realm to make itself known in the earthly realm. Amen.

When My Money Got Funny,
I Didn't Laugh, I Prayed!

I wanted to push the pause button for a bit to focus on finance one more time and go a bit deeper with its connection to my grace experience.

As you recall, I stated earlier that I had no income coming into my household for a solid three months. My savings had already been depleted, and I had one check in my possession to last through the summer. Summers in Houston are brutal, and my electricity averages about $450-$500 every month during the summer. I leaned on Matthew 6:21: *"For where your treasure is, there your heart will be also."* As I looked at my lifestyle, I had convinced myself that it was relatively modest. I was never one who loved expensive jewelry, fancy cars, or lavish trips. I did pour a lot of my resources into my home because I like to entertain family and friends, and cooking is a pure joy for me. I also justified clothing and shoe purchases because I am in the public when I work. I stand in front of groups, so my appearance matters. All of these things in moderation are fine.

The problem I stumbled across was in the consistent tithing that had not been happening over the years. Oh, don't get me wrong; I believe in tithing and have always been a cheerful giver. The problem was in consistency. A retrospective analysis was needed. I thought about when things were really going well, where was I in my worship and tithing? The answer was simple; I was consistent. Problems were encountered, but they were never allowed to become giants that consumed the land and leave scorched earth and remnants of a joy-filled life until now. When the enemy finds a crack, he slips in all his arrogance and sits at your table. As a matter of fact, he never comes alone. He brings his posse. Before you know it, they are gathered around your table and leave you standing there looking for a place to sit. As he went from sitting at the table to pitching a tent, he not only attacked my finances, but he also targeted my marriage. It's like he went shopping and stumbled across a Buy-One-Get-One, the ultimate "two-for" deal.

Something else happened with that one check I was hanging on to for dear life. My estranged husband was in need of help with bills that, honestly, we both were responsible for creating, because that is what happens in a marriage. We always shared our bank accounts, and any purchases with credit cards were made on whatever cards had the available balances. We shared responsibility as we worked as a team, right? Our downfall was that we did not work together as a team in praying over our finances, planning a budget, and tithing responsibly. Again, the enemy is crafty. He saw that opening and barged in with a vengeance.

Well, as I have said, I had one check to last for the duration of the summer. Guess what I did? I shared half of what I had with my husband, even though he had walked out and moved on without me. Before you scream, "What a dummy!" or say anything else to me, just listen to me for a minute and take in the Holy Spirit as I had to do. I had gone to the bank and opened a new account because of the nature of the check. I had planned on just using that as my personal nest egg to tide me over for the summer as best I could.

The problem was that as soon as I got home and was preparing for my new normal routine of dinner alone in front of the television, I was stalked by a voice telling me that I was still a married woman, and everything I had was to be shared with my husband. Yes, even right now. That voice grew louder, and I was unable to sleep. It literally kept me up all night playing the scenario over and over but from the other side. It continuously questioned me: "What if he had the money, and you needed help? How would you feel if he didn't help you? What kind of marriage do you desire?" As the voice grew with persistence,

I said aloud: "Oh boy, could you please be quiet." I could not ignore the simple truth in what I was hearing. Then, I had to focus on one thing I had not heard before...

What kind of marriage do you *want* NOT what kind of marriage do you *have*! Bingo. That was what this was all about. Creating me to be the wife I needed to be for the marriage I desired, not the marriage I currently had. WOW! Praying aloud had become my morning routine, so I prayed aloud for my husband the next morning. As I prayed for him, my words were cut off and replace with a simple twist from "protecting my husband" to "the husband I have prepared for you." Yes, out of my mouth, the Spirit took over and professed to me that I was praying for the husband God had prepared for me. I was stumped.

The next time I saw my husband, I shared with him half of what I had. We talked a bit. Because there was so much tension and anger, the conversation turned to a statement from him to me that, simply put, was this: "I hope you don't think that just because you paid these bills I'm coming home!" He had pure venom in his voice that stung my ears and tore my heart. That was not my intent, but to know that his heart was so hardened towards me that he would place such finality on the destruction of our marriage was beyond what I was able to absorb physically, mentally, emotionally, and yes, spiritually.

Money had never been used in our household by either of us to rule over the other. Where was this coming from? Who was he talking to about this? What kind of advice and counseling was he getting? Other questions ran through my mind in a continuous loop that strung together with no answers to separate them. I couldn't digest what I was hearing or feeling. I was in total disbelief. This was not the man I married. This was the enemy's doing. I had to stay mindful that my husband was overtaken somehow by this stronghold, and I had to remain in prayer over my marriage. I was not going to give up or give in, no matter what it looked like, felt like, or sounded like! I reminded myself that I was a woman of GRIT and a woman of defiant faith. I was not going to allow money to be the gasoline that would burn to ashes what was still standing of our fragile, dismantled marriage. God blessed me before, and He would bless me again. I was not going to fall into the snare of greed and selfishness.

I smiled in response to his statement and mustered up some God-given strength to respond to him. I simply explained that my plan was to help him because we were still married—nothing more and nothing less. Satisfied he got what he came for, he soon departed, and I was confounded. I asked God why He stalked me all night about sharing my tiny fortune. "Why God?" I didn't get any response from the supernatural.

I just resigned myself to adjust to my new routine. I will not lie; there was a deep wound inflicted in me by the words and eyes of the man I still deeply loved. I could see that he was void of any affection for me. I just didn't understand how we got there. I did know that God had the final say, so I held on to that for dear life.

I cannot say it enough; the enemy wants to destroy what means the most to you. He quickly saw the money was not where my heart lay, but he continued the attack in a very specific way. I believe he was trying to drive a wedge between us. You know men are wired to be the provider and protector. The enemy went after that part of my husband. I am not making excuses for choices made by my husband, but you must mature in your walk with God to the point that you understand the very schemes of the enemy. I began to notice that since I was not that upset about the finances, the enemy went that much harder after my husband's heart with a vengeance.

As I moved on into the next few weeks, no more money showed up in the mail. There was no word from my husband, either. However, God began to minister to me through friends. I finally got up the courage to share, not all, but some of what my predicament was and that the financial part was weighing heavy on me. One friend said for me to give her my phone bill, and she would take care of that. Others took me out to eat, saving my precious pennies for other needs around the house. Another friend dropped by one day and left money for me. I was amazed at the outpouring of small acts of kindness that I was receiving which helped me make it through the summer. I prayed for each of those women to be doubly blessed, and I will never forget them.

As I prayed for my finances to be restored and for doors to open up for contracts, I began to feel good that I had shared what money I had with my husband. I realized I was being tested for obedience to God's command. Even when it looked like a foolish proposition, I would humble myself, lean not to my own understanding, and trust God. I still tithed every week. I never missed service, and my zeal for the Word of God increased as did my ability to stand strong on the promises of the Lord. Because I was obedient, I was rewarded. I made it through the entire summer on that remaining portion of my check. Oh yes, some bills were late, and I had to contend with phone calls from various entities. Some of them were so kind and worked with me to defer payments and set up plans without my asking. That was the favor of God and the grace of God at work before my very eyes.

Peace became my umpire. I had peace in the middle of a chaotic summer of strange occurrences. My finances were restored and increased that fall. Yes, I found myself overburdened several times, but I maintained my faith that God's grace would be sufficient to meet all my needs! Oh, how the words from the Bible jumped from the pages, unfolded before my eyes, and illustrated to me the magnificence of the Lord in real-time. I get excited now as I write these words, and I am shouting, "Thank you, Lord, for all that You have done for me! I can never repay You, but I will dedicate my life to You each and every day. For the rest of my natural life, I am Your humble servant." The peace I found in the middle of financial distress was and still is immeasurable, unexplainable, and God-given.

I pray that you find the same peace I found if you are in the middle of a financial attack by the enemy. Oh, hindsight is 20/20, and if only I could go back in time, but I cannot. Family prayer time is so important, and to pray for discernment to be able to identify the enemy in advance is crucial. Nevertheless, nothing is too great for God. I have hope for all things and people connected to me because I have seen many of my prayers answered because I believe that my God is greater than any obstacle I face! I continue to lean on 1 John 4:4: *"Ye are of God, my little children, and have overcome them: because greater is he that is in you than he that is in the world.* I always allow this scripture to breathe life into my soul anytime it is exhausted.

I have much more respect for my financial health. I budget now and save, and my spending is only for the necessities with a very occasional shopping spree that pales in comparison to past sprees. My tithing is stronger than ever, just like my prayer life. I make sure I am covered with corporate worship, and I am connected to women of real faith who give godly advice and are careful not to influence me with their personal opinions. I have goals laid out to improve my credit, make major repairs to the home God blessed me with, and to always keep God first.

My contracts are flowing in at the normal rate but with an increase in value! I began praying to have 5-10 days of work per month, equivalent to 20 days, and God is answering that prayer. I asked for this, so I could dedicate more of my time to working for kingdom building. I am serious about spreading God's word and walking the path He has set before me for His glory. I understand my purpose, my passion, and this is the preparation for my future.

If you are married, do not abandon your marriage without good reason. I stayed in prayer every day for my husband, and I still stay in prayer. I truly believe that God not only hears my prayers, but He is also answering them even as I write this book. I circle my husband each day with prayer even though we are no longer in contact. Who knows; by the end of this book, there may be a praise report waiting for you about my marriage!

With or without *that* praise report showing up by the end of the writing of this book, I give all glory to You, Lord for all that You have done in my life. I am so grateful that You love me enough to cover me with your grace, provide me with unlimited GRIT, and unleash within my soul a defiant faith I never knew I was capable of having.

Pray with me now, as I pray for you.

Heavenly Father, we are reminded in Ecclesiastes 5:10 that *"Whoever loves money never has enough; whoever loves wealth is never satisfied with their income. This too is meaningless."* I come to You now my Holy Father with this reader on my heart. Shield her from the enemy's fiery darts that come upon her finances and relationships. Let her not have a love for money or wealth that is contrary to Your word. Where she is in need, I ask that You make provision and that she be a good steward of what You provide. Be there for her Father to comfort and wipe away every tear and whisper gently to her that she is never alone. Provide spiritual wisdom and discernment so that the enemy is easily recognizable. Let us separate any person in her life that has been overtaken by the enemy and pray for their deliverance back to your protection in Jesus' name! I stand in faith that you will dismantle any guilt, shame, or low self-esteem, right now, Father that contributes to the disruption of her family and relationship harmony. We are joint heirs to Your throne, and I ask you now for her complete access to all that is promised in Your word. I pray that she will be a good and godly steward over the provisions You so graciously give. Thank you, Lord for loving us and breathing life into us. May we usher Your spirit into every dark place and circumstances that we encounter with Your supernatural help, in Jesus' name we pray, Amen. Now, we lift up our eyes, raise our hands, glorify, and thank You for what you have already done according to this prayer petition! All praise, glory, and honor to You, my blessed Savior!

Jesus loves us all, and his death paid for our sins. I had to understand that God's grace was always available to me, and I should not feel ashamed to ask for it or receive it. God is *"no respecter of persons"* (Rom. 2:11). My friend, God, has already done His part; it is now up to us to receive the truth by faith, and make it a reality in our life. Amen!

My Future, His Grace

My beloved reader, I have no idea of what my future will be, but I am trusting God with every single detail of it. Grit means tenacity, and I know that whatever I will encounter, God has given me the tenacity to be successful, and His grace will be sufficient. If I am to succeed in my future, I know I must be intentional and stay committed in love to Jesus as my Lord and Savior.

Scripture reminds me most assuredly of the following:

> *"If I speak in the tongues of men and of angels, but have not to love, I am a noisy gong or a clanging cymbal. And if I have prophetic powers, and understand all mysteries and all knowledge, and if I have all faith, so as to move mountains, but have not to love, I am nothing. If I give away all I have, and if I deliver up my body to be burned but have not love, I gain nothing."* (1 Corinthians 13:1-3)

I can be sure of only one thing about my future, and I am asking you to also place your trust alongside mine with this spiritual fact: God's plan for you and me involve love. Has the Holy Spirit placed a request on your heart and mind? If so, and you are only active in your mind and leave your heart behind, then you are missing the point, my friend. You must desire to be intentionally active in God's plan while loving those who are connected to you whether they are friend or foe. I learned that I must keep my heart engaged in every opportunity I have to do the Lord's work. Remember, *"Love bears all things, believes all things, hopes all things, endures all things. Love never ends."* (1 Corinthians 13:7-8a)

I am also assured that any time in my future that I see a need, and resources are lacking that I will call on God, and He *will* answer the call. Has God has placed a burden on your heart to love children, love the elderly, help feed the hungry, or any area where you can serve others? If so, then answer that call and volunteer. God placed it on my heart to write this book to glorify Him and help others. Over the past year, my prayer life has grown exponentially because God kept connecting me with women who needed prayer for their health, marriage, children, careers, and other needs. While you may reflect on what you have read and not see me as successful in my marriage and not able to clearly advise someone, I would ask that you reconsider. You see, God often calls those who people would deem as unqualified; He makes them qualified according to His unique assignment and instruction. I may not have a perfect marriage, but I am a perfect person to talk to about standing strong in the face of the enemy with tenacity and defiance and not losing my faith, peace, and joy in the midst of a storm! I am the perfect person to talk to about loss, disappointment, heartache, and pain. I can talk about how to circumnavigate those things while staying on the path God desires with joy and praise in the heart and on the lips. I am the perfect one to talk to about the power of faith and prayer and how I have seen healing manifested as the result of prayers!

I understand that when God calls, He is serious. Matthew 25:35-40 says, *"'For I (Jesus) was hungry, and you gave me food, I was thirsty, and you gave me drink, I was a stranger, and you welcomed me, I was naked, and you clothed me, I was sick, and you visited me, I was in prison, and you came to me.' Then the righteous will answer Him, saying, 'Lord, when did we see you hungry and feed you, or thirsty and give you drink? And when did we see you a stranger and welcome you, or naked and clothe you? And when did we see you sick or in prison and visit you? And the King will answer them, 'Truly, I say to you, as you did it to one of the least of these my brothers, you did it to me.'"*

You see, my friend, whenever you serve another person, you are also serving Christ and answering the call. You are being obedient. Matthew 25:41-46 says the exact opposite of the previous passage. It tells of how those who reject the hungry, thirsty, naked, sick, and in prison will also be rejected from entering heaven because rejecting another human being is also rejecting Christ himself. Please answer when God calls! Whenever you ignore His call, you are ignoring Him! Whenever you listen and respond to His call, you are serving Him!

Prayer has been my lifeline, and it is the way to stay connected with God. I believe that any success that I achieve in my future will be a positive correlation to the prayer life that I have established. My communication with God is as active as any line of communication that I have with my best friend on earth. If you are anything like me and sometimes don't know what God's plan is for you, ask Him in prayer. Remember 1 John 5:14-15: *"And this is the confidence that we have toward Him, that if we ask anything according to His will, he hears us. And if we know that He hears us in whatever we ask, we know that we have the requests that we have asked of Him."* I am constantly praying that "God's will be done" in my life. I hope now that you will implement that into your daily prayers if it is not already there. If it is, let the words have meaning. So many of our prayers end up on auto-pilot and lose meaning; they become ritualistic rather than relational. Always ask that God "will" show you your next step in His plan. That is what I am doing for my future because I don't have another minute to waste, do you?

1 Thessalonians 5:17 says to *"pray without ceasing."* While trusting in God to lead me (and you), it is important to stay in constant contact with Him. God still yearns for a relationship with us. When Jesus was praying in Luke 22:42, in the Garden of Gethsemane, He asked God: *"Father, if Thou art willing, remove this cup from Me; yet not My will, but Thine be done."* Jesus did not want to go through the ordeal of the crucifixion, and He asked the Father for a way out. His prayer was not answered the way Jesus requested. Nevertheless, He submitted His will to the will of the Father, and that is the key to prayer. Let us honor Him now in prayer and ask that He will guide us according to His will for our future.

I candidly admit that I am not smart enough to know what to pray for; that's why I must always pray that God's will be done. How often have you looked back over something that you prayed for over and over, and God did not answer only to see later that God's unresponsiveness was really a blessing? Again, His grace and mercy over my future are my security blankets that comfort me when I stand in prayer.

Let us pray.

Our Father, we thank You for Your amazing grace and the ability to rest in Your grace. We desire that Your grace consume our hearts right now as we lift up our voices in prayer. We come to You now asking You to order our steps, as we walk into a future we can neither see nor predict. We place our hands in Yours, for we know You hold the future in Your hands, and what better place for us to seek guidance is there than You? We thank You for the opportunity that You love us so much that we can trust You with our future and know that You will not steer us in the wrong direction. We cannot lean to our own understanding and do not want to make any decisions without Your blessing. Lord, reveal to us anything that we are doing that prevents our prayers from being heard and prevents us from being in Your will. We ask forgiveness for our sins, and we desire to conform in every way to Your purpose and plan for our lives. Right now, Lord, we are in agreement as we ask for You to open our eyes and hearts with these petitions we lay at Your throne and offer them to you in earnest prayer.

Father, I ask that you _____ *(insert your specific request)*

---

if this is in Your will for my life. If it is not in Your will, I pray that You reveal it to me and direct me to what is within Your will. We thank You, Lord, for hearing and answering our prayer according to Your perfect will, in Jesus' name, Amen!

Please read over these scriptures on grace. Select the ones that resonate with you. Copy them on paper, and reflect on why they resonate with you. I there a word, or something about it that connects with a particular issue you are having? Did it just seem to catch your attention? This is how the Holy Spirit talks to us in that quiet whisper.

Some of these scriptures you may turn into prayers if they resonate with a particular challenge you or a loved one is facing, and you desire the grace of God in the situation. I wish I could tell you which scripture will work best for you, but that is when and why we have a prayer life to trust that God will reveal to us just what is needed for every situation.

When you worry and complain, you attract the enemy because he sees your weaknesses, and he strategically targets you! Take those things that give you angst and turn them into positive prayers of victory. God foresaw what is going on in your life, and He prepared these scriptures for you, so use them to fight the battle and declare victory in Jesus' name!

> *2 Corinthians 12:9 - But he said to me, "My grace is sufficient for you, for my power is made perfect in weakness." Therefore, I will boast all the more gladly of my weaknesses, so that the power of Christ may rest upon me.*

Ephesians 2:8-9 - For by grace, you have been saved through faith. And this is not your own doing; it is the gift of God, not a result of works, so that no one may boast.

Romans 6:14 - For sin will have no dominion over you since you are not under law but under grace.

Romans 11:6 - But if it is by grace, it is no longer based on works; otherwise grace would no longer be grace.

James 4:6 - But he gives more grace. Therefore, it says, "God opposes the proud, but gives grace to the humble."

Ephesians 2:8 - For by grace, you have been saved through faith. And this is not your own doing; it is the gift of God,

1 Corinthians 15:10 - But by the grace of God, I am what I am, and his grace toward me was not in vain. On the contrary, I worked harder than any of them, though it was not I, but the grace of God that is with me.

Hebrews 4:16 - Let us then with confidence draw near to the throne of grace that we may receive mercy and find grace to help in time of need.

John 1:16 - And from his fullness we have all received, grace upon grace.

Galatians 2:19-21 - For through the law, I died to the law so that I might live to God. I have been crucified with Christ. It is no longer I who live, but Christ who lives in me. And the life I now live in the flesh I live by faith in the Son of God, who loved me and gave himself for me. I do not nullify the grace of God, for if righteousness were through the law, then Christ died for no purpose.

Hebrews 13:9 - Do not be led away by diverse and strange teachings, for it is good for the heart to be strengthened by grace, not by foods, which have not benefited those devoted to them.

Romans 5:20 - Now the law came in to increase the trespass, but where sin increased, grace abounded all the more,

Acts 20:32 - And now I commend you to God and to the word of his grace, which is able to build you up and to give you the inheritance among all those who are sanctified.

Hebrews 12:15 - See to it that no one fails to obtain the grace of God; that no "root of bitterness" springs up and causes trouble, and by it many become defiled;

1 Peter 4:10 - As each has received a gift, use it to serve one another, as good stewards of God's varied grace:

1 Peter 5:10 - And after you have suffered a little while, the God of all grace, who has called you to his eternal glory in Christ, will himself restore, confirm, strengthen, and establish you.

Genesis 6:8 - But Noah found favor in the eyes of the LORD.

2 Peter 1:2 - May grace and peace be multiplied to you in the knowledge of God and of Jesus our Lord.

1 Peter 5:5 - Likewise, you who are younger, be subject to the elders. Clothe yourselves, all of you, with humility toward one another, for "God opposes the proud but gives grace to the humble."

Acts 15:11 - But we believe that we will be saved through the grace of the Lord Jesus, just as they will."

1 Timothy 6:17 - As for the rich in this present age, charge them not to be haughty, nor to set their hopes on the uncertainty of riches, but on God, who richly provides us with everything to enjoy.

Romans 3:24 - And are justified by his grace as a gift, through the redemption that is in Christ Jesus,

Titus 2:11-14 - For the grace of God has appeared, bringing salvation for all people, training us to renounce ungodliness and worldly passions, and to live self-controlled, upright, and godly lives in the present age, waiting for our blessed hope, the appearing of the glory of our great God and Savior Jesus Christ, who gave himself for us to redeem us from all lawlessness and to purify for himself a people for his own possession who are zealous for good works.

Romans 3:20-24 - For by works of the law, no human being will be justified in his sight since through the law comes knowledge of sin. But now the righteousness of God has been manifested apart from the law, although the Law and the Prophets bear witness to it— the righteousness of God through faith in Jesus Christ for all who believe. For there is no distinction: for all have sinned and fall short of the glory of God, and are justified by his grace as a gift, through the redemption that is in Christ Jesus,

John 1:14 - And the Word became flesh and dwelt among us, and we have seen his glory, glory as of the only Son from the Father, full of grace and truth.

2 Timothy 2:1 - You then, my child, be strengthened by the grace that is in Christ Jesus,

Titus 2:11 - For the grace of God has appeared, bringing salvation for all people,

2 Peter 3:9 - The Lord is not slow to fulfill his promise as some count slowness but is patient toward you, not wishing that any should perish, but that all should reach repentance.

Isaiah 40:31 - But they who wait for the LORD shall renew their strength; they shall mount up with wings like eagles; they shall run and not be weary; they shall walk and not faint.

Ephesians 2:1-22 - And you were dead in the trespasses and sins in which you once walked, following the course of this world, following the prince of the power of the air, the spirit that is now at work in the sons of disobedience— among whom we all once lived in the passions of our flesh, carrying out the desires of the body and the mind, and were by nature children of wrath, like the rest of mankind. But God, being rich in mercy, because of the great love with which he loved us, even when we were dead in our trespasses, made us alive together with Christ— by grace, you have been saved...

2 Timothy 1:9 - Who saved us and called us to a holy calling, not because of our works but because of his own purpose and grace, which he gave us in Christ Jesus before the ages began,

Jude 1:4 - For certain people have crept in unnoticed who long ago were designated for this condemnation, ungodly people, who pervert the grace of our God into sensuality and deny our only Master and Lord, Jesus Christ.

John 1:17 - For the law was given through Moses; grace and truth came through Jesus Christ.

2 Timothy 4:22 - The Lord, be with your spirit. Grace be with you.

2 Corinthians 9:8 - And God is able to make all grace abound to you so that having all sufficiency in all things at all times; you may abound in every good work.

2 Peter 3:18 - But grow in the grace and knowledge of our Lord and Savior Jesus Christ. To him be the glory both now and to the day of eternity. Amen.

Numbers 6:25 - The LORD make his face to shine upon you and be gracious to you;

John 3:16 - "For God so loved the world, that he gave his only Son, that whoever believes in him should not perish but have eternal life.

Ephesians 4:7 - But grace was given to each one of us according to the measure of Christ's gift.

2 Corinthians 8:7 - But as you excel in everything—in faith, in speech, in knowledge, in all earnestness, and in our love for you—see that you excel in this act of grace also.

Colossians 4:2-6 - Continue steadfastly in prayer, being watchful in it with thanksgiving. At the same time, also pray for us, that God may open to us a door for the word, to declare the mystery of Christ, on account of which I am in prison— that I may make it clear, which is how I ought to speak. Walk in wisdom toward outsiders, making the best use of the time. Let your speech always be gracious, seasoned with salt, so that you may know how you ought to answer each person.

Romans 6:1-4 - What shall we say then? Are we to continue in sin that grace may abound? By no means! How can we who died to sin still live in it? Do you not know that all of us who have been baptized into Christ Jesus were baptized into his death? We were buried therefore with him by baptism into death, in order that, just as Christ was raised from the dead by the glory of the Father, we too might walk in newness of life.

Acts 4:33 - And with great power the apostles were giving their testimony to the resurrection of the Lord Jesus, and great grace was upon them all.

Ephesians 2:4-5 - But God, being rich in mercy, because of the great love with which he loved us, even when we were dead in our trespasses, made us alive together with Christ—by grace, you have been saved

Galatians 1:15 - But when he who had set me apart before I was born, and who called me by his grace,

Romans 5:8 - But God shows his love for us in that while we were still sinners, Christ died for us.

CHAPTER 2

What I Learned About Restoration

Restoration is the act of restoring. It is the return of something to a former, original, normal, or unimpaired condition. It can also be restitution of something that was taken away or lost.

As you delve into reading this chapter, I must quickly remind you that we were all born of sin; thus, we naturally have a sinful nature. As I gathered my thoughts on restoration, I had to come to grips with the fact that my original, normal, or unimpaired condition is one of sin. Oh, my. Some people will stop right here and use this a justification for all the wrong they do. You know the excuse: "I was just born that way." God sent Jesus for our redemption, so we have a choice to be restored. It is ours for the asking. However, there is sacrifice and obedience required. Restoration is an ongoing process for me. Each day is a new day, each day a new opportunity, and each day a new challenge. With each day is also an encounter with the enemy who wants me to stumble, fall, and never get up. That is why I must read, study, meditate, and apply the God's word to be restored each day. I have leaned on these scriptures to help me understand what I must intentionally set my mind to do each day:

> *Galatians 2:20 - "I have been crucified with Christ, and it is no longer I who live, but Christ lives in me; and the life which I now live in the flesh I live by faith in the Son of God, who loved me and gave Himself up for me.*

> *Colossians 3:5 - Therefore consider the members of your earthly body as dead to immorality, impurity, passion, evil desire, and greed, which amounts to idolatry.*

> *Ephesians 4:22-24 - ...that, in reference to your former manner of life, you lay aside the old self, which is being corrupted in accordance with the lusts of deceit, and that you be renewed in the spirit of your mind, and put on the new self, which in the likeness of God has been created in righteousness and holiness of the truth.*

> *Luke 9:23 - And He was saying to them all, "If anyone wishes to come after me, he must deny himself, and take up his cross daily and follow me.*

The story of Peter's denials is recorded in the Scripture to underscore two great facts:

1. The weakness and sinfulness of even the most prominent saints, and

2. The greatness and abundance of God's love and grace toward those who fail!

God is the Creator who not only knows every weakness we have, but He also has a remedy for them! That is how much He loves us. He doesn't want us to fail. When we walk with the Lord, we must keep our eyes open because comfort and contentment are often seducers that allow us to let down our guard, and we fall. For any who have fallen, the story of Peter holds out the hope of pardon through God's abundant grace. All you have to do is turn back and reach out to Him, and restoration is yours.

We cannot trust in Christ to save us without repudiating trust in our own efforts to save ourselves. The repentance and faith which save us do not put us in a protective bubble so that we are free from all sin until we get to heaven. The Christian life *begins* with repentance and faith. It also *continues* with repentance and faith on a daily basis whenever we sin or when God's word opens our eyes to sin that we previously were not aware of.

Every day I must repent of my sins and choose to walk in faith if I truly know Christ.

Pray with me now.

Father, You know the areas in my life where I am weak and need to repent. Please reveal them to me. I open my heart to receive your direction on how to pray and how to take active steps to strengthen my heart and mind so that the character I am developing reflects the character of Christ. I wish to follow you; therefore, I deny my fleshly desires that do not align with Your will for my life. I willingly take up your cross, and I lovingly follow you. I know that with you, God, all things are possible, and I humble myself to Your authority over my life. I pray for restoration that only You are powerful enough to deliver unto me. Help me to be gracious, kind, and loving to and with all those I encounter today. I pray that the face of Jesus shines through my every action and word. Help me to deal with my daily difficulties in a way that pleases you, Lord. I humbly and sincerely ask, and thank you for Your grace to lighten any load today that is too much for me to bear, in Jesus' name, Amen.

Restoration - The Prayer and Faith Connection

M y beloved reader, I must be totally candid with you. I found myself in some very difficult situations over the past 13 months, and there were many times that I felt like I was on the cusp of losing my faith. Yes, there were times where I felt like God was not listening or that He simply didn't care! It was in those times I had to train myself to be still and pray. It was in those times I needed to have a group of prayer warriors surrounding me because I was exhausted from the fight. It was in those times I learned to identify the tools the enemy was using to distract me, such as doubt, pity, anger, fear, and unforgiveness, to name a few. I had to remember that *faith is the substance of things hoped for and the evidence of things not [yet] seen. (Hebrews 11:1)* I had to remind myself that there was a power working on my behalf, even when I could not see it. I had to learn to trust, despite my circumstances. I had to learn to hold on to keep my faith intact. I had to make the cognizant choice to believe! Because I hung in there and did not succumb, I was able to achieve a level of GRIT and boldness in my faith that I now share with you.

**First, I unlocked the power and potential of my prayer
life.** I began to set aside time for daily prayer that was focused
on scripture readings and applications. I began to receive
scriptures as I prayed for specific areas in my life. Those
scriptures helped me to persevere because it was tangible
evidence that God was listening to me.

One of the most triumphant prayer focal points was when
I labored over Luke 2:52 for 52 days. Each day, I began by
reading that particular scripture: *"As Jesus grew in wisdom,
stature, and favor with God and man ..."* I began to pray that
scripture over myself in the following way:

As Jesus grew in wisdom, stature, and favor with God
and man so must I. I make this body a temple for Jesus
to reside in. I welcome You into my very existence
and ask that You grow in me because You live in me.
I desire to increase in wisdom, for it is the foundation
for all things that are to come. I will be prepared for
the stature and positions that will be mine because I am
asking You, Lord, to open doors of opportunity for me
in every aspect of my life. I ask You, Lord for favor as
the doors are opened, for any door You open no man can
shut. I also ask that You shut all doors that are not for
me, and I desire the spiritual discernment to know when

You have shut a door. I desire to serve You, Lord, all the days of my life. Any wealth You provide me with, I will share and I devote my life to serving You, Father, on this earth. I am Your empty vessel. Pour Your life and light into me so that I may draw others unto You. I understand my purpose, and I humble myself to serve You and You alone. Equip me, Lord, for the journey with GRIT. I trust You, and I thank You in Jesus' name, Amen.

I changed up my prayer somewhat over the 52 days, but this was the cornerstone prayer. I prayed for a revelation of those who were actively working to destroy my marriage. I prayed for the restoration of my finances and to be debt free. I prayed for those who were my enemy. I connected myself with a few prayer lines on a regular basis. I even began to lead the prayer line for my church as a result of this season. Through praying for others, I was able to take the focus off myself and serve others. I began to hear praise reports of those we had prayed for, and that made my heart sing with joy. I stayed in a positive place with my prayer life, even though it seemed God was not answering my prayers for healing and restoration in my marriage. I began to understand that His way was not my way. As I prayed, I was ordered to be still, wait, pray, don't give up hope on my husband or my marriage, and keep moving forward! Wow, I had to pray on how to do all that simultaneously. However, this is where my prayer for wisdom kicked in.

I began to pray to be transformed into the minister God desired me to be, the wife I needed to be for the husband that God promised me, and to be the mother and grandmother I needed to be as an example for the next generation. I stopped being so laser-focused on one dimension and expanded my prayers to cover every facet of my life. I began to understand how to pray, even though my personal situation seemed to be unchanging, because I allowed God authority over my heart, thoughts, and actions. I began to enhance my prayer time with listening to sermons and pouring the Word of God into me. I was so fragile, and I knew it. If I would have allowed the wrong messaging to permeate my physical space, it would have had a negative influence on me. I did not become a "holy roller," but I was restored through the process. I had lost my joy, but it was returned to me. I had lost hope, but it was returned to me. I had lost peace, but it was returned to me. All returned, all restored because I humbled myself to God's process, and turned my pain into prayer and purpose!

Organizing for Prayer Time

M y consistent prayer life unlocked my faith and my purpose. My purpose gave me a plan. My faith is what I needed to see the plan through to fruition. The plan was to *organize* for prayer time. It had to become an integral part of my life. For Christians, prayer should be like breathing. You do not have to think to breathe because the atmosphere exerts pressure on your lungs and essentially forces you to breathe. That is why it is more difficult to hold your breath than it is to breathe. Similarly, when we are born into the family of God, we enter into a spiritual atmosphere where God's presence and grace exert pressure, or influence, on our lives. That pressure and influence fuels faith. Prayer is the normal response to that pressure. As I went through this restoration process, I also saw that same grace exerting pressure on me to influence others as they watched my faith grow and mature. God did not want me to keep all this to myself!

Each of us is different. How we pray and develop our relationship with God is a very personal and intimate process. I am sharing with you what worked for me. It may be confirmation for some readers and a good outline for others.

65

I know whatever you do, making time for God should be the ultimate goal. That is what He desires, and it will please Him. The residual is you will find an increase in your faith because God will begin to speak to you regularly because you made time for him in your life.

1. Make Time.

I did not set aside a specific time of day, but I did make time each day and learned the importance of starting there first to get off on the right foot. Here are some of the power steps that I took:

- Begin with gratitude. I am so thankful that God loves me enough to allow me the relationship I have with Him. I don't have to schedule an appointment. I can talk with Him anytime, about anything, and for as long a time as I need. Starting with gratitude has heightened my consciousness of the little things that God has done that might slip under my radar. It also creates great opportunities for me to trust Him.

- Incorporate prayer into everyday chores. I used to think I had to stop and drop everything in order to pray. I now find myself just calling on the name of Jesus throughout the day. I sing songs I make up. Some are actually scriptures I want to commit to memory, so I set them to melody. I find that a peace ensues when I do this, and that awareness is intoxicating. It pushes away all negative aspects of my day throughout the day.

○ Tell Him what He already knows. I had to just get real and spill it all out, and it made me feel so much better. My natural rhythm was to take care of my problems, hide my hurt, and not be transparent to anyone, including God. I wanted to stand before God and pray with a perfect-wrong approach. I now tell Him everything. I am completely honest about what still hurts and what I would like to just go away. I even laugh sometimes because I tell Him, "I know you won't erase it, but I had to put it out there just in case you were feeling like tossing a miracle my way today!" Taking this approach has helped me to relieve stress, release anxiety, and remove frustration with the process. It helps to maintain my peace.

○ Pray while you wait. Ah, this is the hard part—but it is the classroom. I know how to immediately begin to pray in all situations. Some people wait until there's nothing else they can do, and then they pray. If they had moved prayer to the forefront, the challenge might never have grown roots. Even if it did, there would be a greater sense of contentment because God was put at the helm of the storm's onset.

○ Sing a song of praise. Pray and then praise. I learned that once I had delivered my prayer to stop pleading my case, and just thank God for His answer. His time is not my time. Patience was developed in the process. Wisdom was developed in the process. An authentic relationship with God was born through praise.

○ When you mess up, admit it. Oh, there were days when I was tired, I skipped my prayer time. There were also times I heard from the Holy Spirit and only acted on part of what was told to me because I doubted or felt that there was a better alternative. Am I sorry? Yes, I am because that was an act of disobedience. I was quick to recognize it and ask for forgiveness. God is a merciful father who doesn't want to see us fail. Therefore, He always has a second chance for us. He has an unlimited supply of mercy and grace for us. He is waiting to make it available.

○ Give up worrying. Worry or anxiety is negative faith. Replaying what went wrong does not change anything, but it releases negative energy that the enemy will use to distract you. It can make a small error in judgment seem so unredeemable that you give up, and that is just what the enemy wants you to do!

○ Stop talking once in a while. Instead, just listen. Need I say more?

2. Study.

I also dedicated myself to one hour of reading and studying the Bible each day. This was tremendous a support, and it facilitated a deeper understanding of the scriptures. That wisdom I was praying for was showing up, and my spiritual foundation was being poured. In my study, I gained a better understanding of how to pray and the meaning of prayer. You see, I wanted to know more about it, and God showed me just what I needed. It unlocked my eyes and heart to the real power of prayer.

Through study, I developed a depth of understanding that surpassed the shallow understanding I had long held of various scriptures. For example, I gained a much more insightful understanding of Paul's command in 1 Thessalonians 5:17 to *"pray without ceasing."* At first, I found this confusing because of the physical position of praying that I had been raised to use each time I prayed. You know, head bowed, or on my knees. Obviously, this scripture cannot mean we are to be in a head-bowed, eyes-closed posture all day long! Paul is not referring to non-stop talking, but rather an attitude of God-consciousness and God-surrender that we carry with us all the time. Every waking moment is to be lived in an awareness that God is with us and that He is actively involved and engaged in our thoughts and actions.

Study also revealed to me that when my thoughts turn to worry, fear, discouragement, and anger, I needed to consciously and quickly turn every thought into prayer and every prayer into thanksgiving. In his letter to the Philippians, Paul commands us to stop being anxious and instead, *"in everything, by prayer and petition, with thanksgiving, present your requests to God."* (Philippians 4:6) He taught the believers at Colossae to devote themselves *"to prayer, being watchful and thankful."* (Colossians 4:2) Paul exhorted the Ephesian believers to see prayer as a weapon to use in fighting spiritual battles. (Ephesians 6:18) As I grew in my understanding of this scripture, I understood the benefit of why prayer should be my first response to every fearful situation, every anxious thought, and every undesired task that God commands. In retrospect, I saw how a lack of prayer caused me to depend on myself instead of depending on God's grace. A lack of prayer resulted in a diminished faith. Unceasing prayer became, in essence, my new weapon of choice. I submitted to God and accepted that I needed the continual dependence upon and communion with the Father. This allowed me to grow my faith exponentially.

3. Rest on The Promises of God.

I had to go beyond my situation and look to the One from whom my help comes! I understood that I would never be successful—never be restored—in this fight because I was never meant to be in it alone! I had to search the Scripture, find promises that related to my situation, and start praying them. Then I had to trust God to bring them to pass in my life. I had to learn how to pray God's promises and how to speak His life into myself and my situation. We must understand one simple truth—In order to see fulfillment of the promises of God, we need to first come to terms with the fact that these promises are available specifically to us! He wants to fulfill His promises in our lives. However, that doesn't mean we don't have a part to play in their fulfillment; we need to believe His promises and confess them. I had to move from pleading my case to presenting my case! My prayers at first were pleas for God to step in, and just make things happen for me. With the wisdom I gained through study and prayer, I began to understand that prayer is strategic, not random. This understanding expanded my relationship with God. It made Him not just the head but the center of my life.

I wrote my prayers out but wrote them in terms of God's promises. I wanted God to know that I expected Him to fulfill His promises because Scripture tells me that God is not a man that He should lie. Praying with the Scripture effectively escorted the enemy away from my life and my situations. I began to focus on speaking the living word into dead situations and allowing God to show His power. My faith blossomed each time I did this. I came to the altar with an expectation for victory and praying according to His will. As always, I turned scriptures into prayers. I wanted to keep track of my prayers and be able to thank God for victories as they were answered and also show evidence of God's faithfulness when we diligently seek Him. Here is one of my examples of Scripture turned into a prayer:

Scripture

> *Ephesians 5:25-26 - Husbands, love your wives, just as Christ loved the church and gave himself up for her to make her holy, cleansing her by the washing with water through the word,*

My Prayer Request

> Lord, You have a divine plan for my marriage, and I am presenting to Your words to You and praying

for the manifestation of Your will in my marriage. I know that You know what is best for me, and I pray this according to Your will for my life. I come to You now, humble and with a grateful heart because I know You love me.

I pray that God's voice through the Holy Spirit will remind my beloved husband of how to love me and teach him how to love me as Christ loved the church. I pray that his love for me is a hearty love, an enduring love, a fervent love, and an intense love that is not lip service but heart serviced! I pray that my husband will delight in me as his wife, and he will prize my affection. Daily I will pray that you, my beloved husband, will be sanctified, set apart from the world, and daily conformed more and more to the image of God's Son. Glory to glory! Be transformed by the Holy Spirit. Be cleansed, my husband, so that your cleansing will cleanse me. Your covering will cover me. Let the living waters flow through you and into me, for we are one vessel now. What you allow into you is also manifested in me. Prepare your heart daily, my husband, for God's entry. Because I am the weaker vessel, cover me with your undying Christ-like love that will be given to you as you offer yourself daily to God as a living sacrifice. I surrender and submit to my husband, dear Lord, for he has submitted himself to You. This divine relationship we have in the spiritual realm will soon be manifested in the earthly realm. I thank You now, for it is already done! What God has joined together, let no man put asunder! I rest this petition at Your altar. I thank you Lord for the complete restoration of our marriage because I have prayed according to your plan, God's plan, for marriage. I receive the victory, and I receive the restoration in Jesus' name, Amen!

I was blessed with a powerful prayer partner who was also a woman of GRIT. She mentored me and held me accountable for my prayer time and kept me focused. When I wanted to have a pity party, she would allow me time to vent, but quickly redirected my negative energy to positive energy!

The bottom line for prayer for me was to have an accountability partner, to be consistent in daily prayer, and to serve others by praying for them. Because of my commitment to prayer, my faith was nourished and was on full display for the world to see. I have stood firm on my faith that God will answer my prayers because He planted each one in my heart with His mighty hand. My faith will bring each prayer to harvest. I already see a mighty forest that stands in testament to my faith that what God planted in my heart will grow!

As you go through a trying experience, never underestimate the power of prayer! If you have a strong prayer life now, work to increase it by praying actively for others. The enemy never sleeps. He is strategic and has surgical precision in his attacks. Your prayer life is your ultimate weapon. Develop it. Use it. Share it.

Create a list of your prayer life goals:

I want to continue_____

I want to improve_____

I want to learn more about _____

The scriptures I will study and use to pray on are_____

4. Always Focus on Gratitude in the Restoration Process.

It was so tempting to wallow in self-pity, and who would have blamed me? However, I knew that as a woman of GRIT, pity was not the place I wanted to pitch my tent and dwell. I had to consciously release the spirit of pessimism from my soul and replace it with optimism. I had to vet the people I wanted to confide in because I did not to find myself in that negative echo chamber with doubters and people who did not believe in restoration and deliverance. You see, praying for my husband and my marriage was novel to many people.

We live in a society where when you tire of someone or something, the easy way out is to walk away and replace it, or just talk yourself into a state of mind where you believe it wasn't valuable, to begin with. Well, I am not that foolish where I want to entertain such nonsense. I value relationships. I value people. I am not the fixer, but I am someone who will stand in the gap and pray. I needed to be mindful each day of all the gifts I had been given and to cherish them. I learned to be grateful and began to journal about my daily gifts.

I would thank God aloud as I prayed for what He had allowed to happen to my life. I saw all the strife and confusion for the gifts that they were—gifts that brought me in such close proximity to God that I could hear His whisper in my ear! I was grateful for the downloading of scriptures that were the channel the Holy Spirit used to speak directly to me to guide me. I had to learn to be still and listen. For this, I was grateful. I looked at my failures, not as failures but lessons.

I asked God each day to help me see the lesson I needed to learn. Of course, I had stumbled and had some serious hiccups along the way. But as a woman of GRIT, I knew that I had to keep moving through the valley of this season, knowing God was in control and on my side. I am grateful that He loved me enough to usher me through the process with angels as my escorts!

My Beloved Reader

What are you grateful for today? Take time to journal and thank God for it. Sometimes it helps to see the things on paper because your vision through eyes of uncertainty, pain, and confusion have a tendency to paint a false picture and leave you feeling hopeless rather than grateful.

Today I am grateful for_____

_____

_____

_____

_____

_____

5. Seek out a Community of Believers and Prayer Warriors.

I needed to connect and hold on to corporate prayer and worship. In the disillusionment of my trials, it would have been so very easy to throw in the towel and walk away from church. The enemy wants you to do just that. If he can cut those ties, he knows you are left outside in the cold, and you will turn to any warm thing for comfort. I did have to stop talking to most of my friends about the details of what was going on because their reactions and advice was not godly and did not align with what I knew I had been told by God. I do understand that not everyone wants to hear about my relationship with God. Not only that, but for some people, this idea that God is speaking to me is very foreign and difficult to digest. I cannot get someone to understand this if his or her relationship with God is not in a place or space that would allow for this to be understood.

I had to stand my ground and get grounded with other like-minded believers. I needed people to pray with me, who were in agreement. Otherwise, the prayers would have been hindered by disbelief and unbelief. The covering of the corporate church helped me to understand the Word of God as I attended service and took a very analytical approach to my note-taking. I began to see connections between sermons and my prayers and the scriptures I was being given during my quiet time.

The church family I have was nonjudgmental and caring during that time. They understood their role was to pray with and for me and to support me in any way possible. Just the sharing of kind words, smiles, and honest inquiries about my wellbeing were medicine to my soul.

My prayer warriors were always on call, and there for me. Even with their support, I had to learn to be alone. There were times I believed God had just shut down all communications and kept me in a quiet space with only Him to talk to. I had many droughts where I couldn't pay someone to answer the phone for a prayer call. I would call, and no one would answer. I would text and no response. I would leave messages only to get return calls days later. I had to learn to notice what God was up to in these times and not get agitated with my prayer partners for not being there for me. You know, they have a life too, and I had to honor that. One more thing, always cover your prayer partners and faith community in prayer. The enemy wants to shut down prayer because he knows the power of prayer.

To Do List:

- Make a list of people you can count on to pray with you and for you.

- Make yourself available to people as a person who will pray for them.

- Cover your church and faith community in prayer each pay.

- If you are not connected to a faith group, pray to God for guidance in securing one.

6. Reflect.

I learned the value of reflective practices as an integral part of the learning process. This valley in which I still find myself in is like a PhD-level course of life. The implementation of reflective practices has allowed me to learn more about myself and improve how to appropriately develop and use my spiritual gifts, tools, and skills. If this is not making sense to you, just for a minute, consider sports teams that watch film of the previous night's game. The purpose is to replay and watch for errors, mistakes and also to learn from what worked well and capitalize on it next time. I don't know about you, but I do not want to keep repeating these valley experiences. I know I will go through more valleys, but each time I go through, I should be better prepared and better equipped. God has given us spiritual gifts to use. God has also given us His word to study and apply. As I go through this valley, I am reflecting on how I handled situations. What worked and didn't work? Did I use my gifts and tools appropriately? I know when I did the right thing because I don't have anxiety about it. I have peace, and as I have said before, peace is my umpire. It is as Philippians 4:7 puts it— "a *peace that surpasses all understanding.*"

Although reflection may be a cumbersome and time-consuming practice to employ, without reflection, it is almost impossible for actual "learning" to occur. Have you ever looked at someone who seems to be repeating the same mistakes in life over and over again? It's like that person has "forgotten" what he or she should have "learned" the last time, but in reality, never really learned it at all. That person simply went *through* a life event in the valley. 2 Peter 2:16 talks about the dog that returns to its vomit. While that may not be exactly what I am referring to here with the inability to reflect, it does paint a graphic picture of how one is doomed to go back and pick up the waste that should have released and walked away from.

Due to my background in education, I am reminded of John Dewey's famous quote, "We don't learn from experience. We learn from reflecting on experience." I am so glad that the God I serve saw fit to equip me with a toolkit that is transferable between my career and my life applications. I realized as I go through my valley experience, the goal God has for me is not merely to get through it, make it, or to come out of it. He wants me to actually learn something that I will need to pick up for later use when I need to transfer it to a new situation. I now know that reflection is no longer optional—it's an essential piece to transition from one valley experience to another. My GRIT is being developed and expanded each time. You know what they say, new levels of new devils!

After all, if I touch a hot stove and burn my hand, but never make the connection that the hot stove is what burned my hand, I'm likely to repeat that mistake. If I pray to God for direction, and He gives me direction, His direction will not help if it doesn't make sense to me. I would rather do it my way; after all, I have all this education and training and have seen others do this and be successful. I am going to ignore God this time and do it my way. That is called disobedience. There is no reward for disobedience, but there is a consequence. You may think, "Of course it's the stove that burned my hand. The stove is an absurd example" Oftentimes in life "What went wrong?" is a question without an obvious answer. Unfortunately, it's a question that the vast majority of people never even think to ask. They prefer to blame someone else for their failure. That is the easiest way out of responsibility, and there is no learning taking place.

Action Steps: Use the following steps to create your own reflective journal as you or someone you know walks through a valley experience. There's no right or wrong way to journal.

The most important thing is to reflect on and learn from this experience. I hope this helps you to start.

- Journal what happens in real-time each day if possible.

- Consider your reactions, feelings, and thoughts about the experiences of the day. What experiences gave you positive or negative emotions? Were you in control of those experiences, or did someone else control them? How were you physically, spiritually, and/or emotionally affected?

- Identify scriptures that align with your feelings. For example, if you were worried, find scriptures that deal with worry, and create a prayer using those scriptures.

- Draw conclusions about choices you made and how that affected you or the situation. For example, if you lost your temper, what could you have done to prevent that, or how could you have diffused the situation and maintained control?

- Develop a plan of action, using prayer and praise points. Write out prayers for comfort or healing, and always find something to praise God for through your journaling experience. Praise is the weapon the enemy hates most!

7. Trust the Process to Strengthen You.

This was one of the most difficult lessons in self-restraint I have had to endure. I am a successful career woman who is used to making decisions and following through on commitments. I make sure I am knowledgeable about the areas for which I create seminars. I am a problem solver and a good one. When I found myself in this valley, I just wanted to fix it. If I couldn't fix it, I honestly wanted it to go away. Does anybody else feel what I am saying right now?

Well, of course, neither of those worked, and I can hear my prayer partner's words echoing in my ear right now: "You have to trust God and trust the process." Oh, how many times was I going to have to endure the repetition of that sentence! I got to a point where I could predict where, in her conversation, it would be interjected! But she was absolutely correct. I had to trust God and trust the process. Trust—a small word with a big shadow. How was I ever going to restore and strengthen my faith, family, and finance while I trusted a process I couldn't even understand at a superficial level? I saw no immediate tangible results in my prayers and obedience. I believed and truly trusted God. After all, I was doing all the right things!

I will say this again; God wanted a relationship with me and not one of ritualistic compliance. Relationships take time.

Trust the process, woman of GRIT! Proverbs 3:5-6 tells us, *"Trust in the LORD with all your heart and lean not on your own understanding; in all your ways submit to him, and he will make your paths straight."* WOW! I was leaning to my own understanding instead of letting go and allowing God to take the reins. My book sense was no match for spiritual warfare, wherein I found myself engaged.

In this valley experience, I learned many valuable lessons. One simple yet important lesson was that everyone who walks with the Lord experiences some kind of spiritual development process. While there have been seasons in my life filled with apparent victory over major sin, with little suffering, and seemingly unhindered communion with God, I was not equipped for what happened this time. I had never really been tested. In this season there was great defeat, loss, affliction, and silence. In this season, this valley – I will once again be completely transparent – I felt tempted to surrender and give up. As I spent time reading and studying the Bible and talking with my prayer partner, I began to understand from God's word (not my perspective) that this is all part of a process, namely the process of sanctification. Having redeemed me from the grave, God was now transforming me and changing me into the image of Jesus. I can remember praying: "Create in me a new creature through Christ Jesus. Prepare me for the husband that you have prepared for me so that I will be the wife he needs, and I can fulfill the ministry assignment you have for me, Lord!" Yes, this was my actual prayer. I asked to be made a new creature, and boy did I get it!

Sanctification is a team effort. Hebrews 10:25-25 encourages us, the people of God, *"to stir up one another to love and good works, not neglecting to meet together, as is the habit of some, but encouraging one another, and all the more as you see the Day drawing near."* This is why my prayer partners and my fellowship in my church was so important. Part of trusting the process is to entrust ourselves to those who are also in the process. This is also why I now make myself available to pray with others who are in the valley while I am still in the valley. It is why I am now writing this book. I can't wait until I am out of the valley to write this; it has to be done now to show that the process can bring forth good fruit! Once again, I'm reminded of God's word that this is all part of a process, namely the process of sanctification.

I may not be able to see all that God is doing, but I am trusting in the process. I know little by little He will reveal, and then it will all make sense. In the process, my patience was strengthened; my resilience was honed; my understanding of the Word of God was magnified; my prayer life was solidified, and I found joy and peace. These things, my beloved reader, are invaluable gifts from the Creator himself who knew just what this woman of GRIT needed! I have a legacy to leave my children and grandchildren so that the generations to come are grounded in the Word of God through His word and my example. Am I perfect? No. Nonetheless, I strive toward being Christ-like every day. Of that, I am so very proud, and I pray that my God is pleased.

I wrote this prayer for myself, and now I share it with you, my beloved reader.

Father, I come to You now with Your words in my heart. In the 23rd Psalm You remind me that You are my shepherd, and because of that, I shall not want for anything. You take me to green pastures and still waters where restoration of my soul may occur. You lead me in the path of righteousness because You love me, and I thank you for it! Right now, I am walking through a dead, lifeless time in my life, but I will fear no evil because I know You are with me. Your rod and staff comfort me. I know You are fending off the enemy that I can neither see nor touch, but You know where he lies, and You will protect me. I trust You, Lord, for the victory, and I know that You are preparing me for a victorious feast of plenty, and my enemies will live to see Your glory. You have covered me in the precious blood of Jesus, and abundance is my inheritance. Your goodness and mercy will forever follow me, and I have comfort in Your bosom as I have refuge in You, Lord. In your presence I will dwell. In me, I make You my king forever!

As I come to You, Father, I also know that your ways are not my ways. I trust You with the process as I walk through this valley, for You know what is best for me. I humble myself to the situation and allow You to have Your way. Create in me a new creature through Christ Jesus. I want to walk like Christ and love like Christ. I want to live a life that honors You, my Heavenly Father, so that you will dwell in me. I thank You for the process. I thank You that my prayer life is growing stronger each day. I thank You that my faith is increasing each day. I thank You that my awareness of Your presence is so keen that I now hear Your voice! I praise you for the victory that is already won; the feast awaits my arrival! I glorify You, O' Lord, and I desire to be used by You to help others through their valley process. I thank You for restoration. In Jesus' name I pray. Thank you, Lord, for hearing and answering my prayer. All praises to You, Lord, Amen.

Scriptures for Restoration

Review these scriptures. Take several of them and turn them into prayers for restoration in areas of your life where you want God's hand to cover you.

> *Joel 2:25-26 - I will restore to you the years that the swarming locust has eaten, the hopper, the destroyer, and the cutter, my great army, which I sent among you. "You shall eat in plenty and be satisfied, and praise the name of the Lord your God, who has dealt wondrously with you. And my people shall never again be put to shame.*

> *Jeremiah 30:17 - For I will restore health to you, and your wounds I will heal, declares the Lord because they have called you an outcast: 'It is Zion, for whom no one cares!'*

> *Psalm 51:12 - Restore to me the joy of your salvation and uphold me with a willing spirit.*

> *Isaiah 61:7 - Instead of your shame there shall be a double portion; instead of dishonor they shall rejoice*

in their lot; therefore, in their land, they shall possess a double portion; they shall have everlasting joy.

Job 42:10 - And the Lord restored the fortunes of Job when he had prayed for his friends. And the Lord gave Job twice as much as he had before.

Acts 3:19-21 - Repent therefore, and turn again, that your sins may be blotted out, that times of refreshing may come from the presence of the Lord, and that he may send the Christ appointed for you, Jesus, whom heaven must receive until the time for restoring all the things about which God spoke by the mouth of his holy prophets long ago.

1 Peter 5:10 - And after you have suffered a little while, the God of all grace, who has called you to his eternal glory in Christ, will himself restore, confirm, strengthen, and establish you.

1 John 5:4 - For everyone who has been born of God overcomes the world. And this is the victory that has overcome the world—our faith.

Mark 11:24 - Therefore I tell you, whatever you ask in prayer, believe that you have received it, and it will be yours.

Revelation 21:1-5 - Then, I saw a new heaven and a new earth, for the first heaven and the first earth had passed away, and the sea was no more. And I saw the holy city, new Jerusalem, coming down out of heaven from God, prepared as a bride adorned for her husband. And I heard a loud voice from the throne saying, "Behold, the dwelling place of God is with man. He will dwell with them, and they will be his people, and God himself will be with them as their God. He will wipe away every tear from their eyes, and death shall be no more, neither shall there be mourning, nor crying, nor pain anymore, for the former things have passed away." And he who was seated on the throne said, "Behold, I am making all things new." Also, he said, "Write this down, for these words are trustworthy and true."

Zechariah 9:12 - Return to your stronghold, O prisoners of hope; today, I declare that I will restore to you double.

Jeremiah 29:11 - For I know the plans I have for you, declares the Lord, plans for welfare and not for evil, to give you a future and a hope.

John 14:1 - Let not your hearts be troubled. Believe in God; believe also in me.

Galatians 6:1 - Brothers, if anyone is caught in any transgression, you who are spiritual should restore him in a spirit of gentleness. Keep watch on yourself, lest you too be tempted.

Matthew 6:33 - But seek first the kingdom of God and his righteousness, and all these things will be added to you.

Isaiah 42:1-25 - Behold my servant, whom I uphold, my chosen, in whom my soul delights; I have put my Spirit upon him; he will bring forth justice to the nations. He will not cry aloud or lift up his voice, or make it heard in the street; a bruised reed he will not break, and a faintly burning wick he will not quench; he will faithfully bring forth justice. He will not grow faint or be discouraged till he has established justice in the earth, and the coastlands wait for his law. Thus, says God, the Lord, who created the heavens and stretched them out, who spread out the earth and what comes from it, who gives breath to the people on it and spirit to those who walk in it: ...

Hosea 6:1 - "Come, let us return to the Lord; for he has torn us, that he may heal us; he has struck us down, and he will bind us up.

James 5:16 - Therefore, confess your sins to one another and pray for one another, that you may be healed. The prayer of a righteous person has great power as it is working.

CHAPTER 3

Integrity

Temptation is tailor made according to your desires. Some days I found it so easy to be lured into the temptation of bitterness and anger because I was rejected and hurting. I wanted God to remove me from my valley. Of course, God did not remove me because the valley was where I was to grow. I had a choice. Either I could grow down and never reach my full potential, grow out and simply keep the same habits, mindsets, and beliefs, or grow up and become the woman of GRIT that God intended for me to be all along. Just like God saw in Noah what He was looking for, God saw in me the qualities He wanted me to grow into, and one of those qualities was integrity. Just like Noah was obedient to the calling God placed on him, I wanted to be obedient. I have friends who don't understand why I do some of the things I do, or why I have the faith I have, but they all say this: "One thing I know about her is that she listens to God!"

Who do you know that can say that about you? I arrived at this road of integrity late in life, but I arrived nonetheless, and so can you if you have not yet done so. If you have, you must also stay the course.

Instead of clothes, cars, and cash, I want to be a woman rich in integrity and godly qualities. On this earth, so much stock is placed on wealth and class, but that means nothing spiritually. Oh, there is nothing wrong with having it, but if that is all you have amassed at the end of life's journey, then your life was a waste. Integrity is one of the legs of the table of the legacy I am building that I desire to leave behind me on this earth. Integrity is what allows me to fully utilize any amount of wealth and exercise the muscle of class in a manner that will glorify God!

> Matthew 5:16 KJV - "Let your light so shine before men, that they may see your good works, and glorify your Father which is in heaven."

Once I learned to listen, trust, and obey the Lord, the fruit I bore was watered with integrity. Warning for the reader: People living in sin don't like these qualities, and those in sin won't like to be around people of integrity, so get ready for the haters! No matter who is around me, I have a made-up mind, and I'm walking in the light of God. Light and dark cannot co-exist. Light will drive out the dark lest I allow the dark to consume me and extinguish my light. I have to be methodical and calculating each day, asking God to order my steps, my words, and my actions so that I will be able to walk upright in integrity, and let His light shine.

As a woman of GRIT, I learned that I must walk differently. Peter writes in 2 Peter 1:2-11 that we should add to our faith virtue, and to virtue knowledge, and to knowledge self-control, and to self-control perseverance, and to perseverance godliness, and to godliness brotherly kindness, and to brotherly kindness—love. If these things are ours, then we will be fruitful in the knowledge of Jesus. As you practice the above things, I believe you will grow in integrity and the knowledge of Jesus. You will be blessed in the way that I was. You will allow godly changes in your life and in the lives of your children as a result. Make it a habit to listen, trust, and obey. These are the actions that will attract people to the God who resides in you. Remember, negative thoughts can keep you from God's best. God can use you as a rainbow to those in a storm, showing what God's transformational grace and mercy does only if He is granted access as the sovereign ruler over anyone's life. Integrity forced my relationship with God to overshadow what I wanted it to be and allowed it to be what He desired all along. In the valley, I found that I needed to know God intimately, and my greatest gifting is that I now know and am known by Him!

The purity and sincerity of God's love revealed to me that it's possible to get what you want and loose what you need! Now, I pray now with Proverbs 3:5 at the center of my prayers that God's will be done in my life, and I trust Him by leaning not to my own understanding. Victory and success are undeniably mine if I follow the Lord, but they will not be quick according to my time. God knows if He gave it all to me instantaneously, I would be consumed by the beast. There's always the release of the beast when you're uncovered and elevated. Then you're a target, and the beast will probably consume everything associated with you! That is why integrity is the bedrock of a successful walk through the valley. My character was being developed, and I had to learn to adhere to God's principles of behavior.

I have to walk with God little by little every single day. This way I remember that success is not mine, but it is because of my God. My God is still my God because I have walked in integrity with Him every day! Thank You, Lord, for loving me for who I am and not what I am.

The road to living with integrity taught me one more thing about obedience: God working daily in the small results in the big things in your life!

What are you struggling with in the area of living with integrity? Bring it to the altar of God and leave it there.

Pray with me now.

Father today, I commit my life to You, and I trust You, LORD, with all my heart and do not rely on my own understanding. I know You know what and who is best for me. I have my wants, but I know that You will provide my needs. Let me not place my wants above what I need. Give me the wisdom, Father, to know and accept what You desire for me because that is what is best for me. I desire to live in integrity and serve You with a sound mind and live by Your principles and exemplify the character of Your Son, Jesus. Father, strengthen me in the area (s) of_____

_____ so that my life is not overshadowed by disobedience and corruption. I am lacking direction with _____; show me the path You have prepared for me. Thank you, Lord, for hearing my prayer. I praise You now for answering my prayer, and I will glorify You and spread Your word, in Jesus' name, Amen.

Leading with Integrity

As a woman of GRIT, I find that I have been catapulted into leadership, my church, home, friendships, and workplace. The Bible has much to say about spiritual integrity, honesty, and living a blameless life. Living a blameless life does not mean there is no sin. It also speaks of sincerity, loyalty, obedience, character, and maintaining consistency under pressure. These qualities are all prerequisites for Christian leadership as well as leadership in any arena where you must lead.

God calls us to another way—one of integrity. So, what does integrity *really* look like?

The Bible and Integrity

The Bible is somewhat silent on the actual term *integrity*. There are a handful of proverbs, such as Proverbs 10:9 and Proverbs 11:3, that mention integrity in certain translations, but most of them are of the "it's good to have integrity because those without it are of the wicked persuasion."

Scripture is *filled*, however, with passages urging integrity in believers—it just talks about integrity without using that term. Think of the most famous New Testament commands for Christian living: *"But the fruit of the Spirit is love, joy, peace, forbearance, kindness, goodness, faithfulness, gentleness, and self-control. Against such things, there is no law. Those who belong to Christ Jesus have crucified the flesh with its passions and desires. Since we live by the Spirit, let us keep in step with the Spirit."* (Galatians 5:22-25) Such a list is a command to live a life of the *highest* integrity, a life that brings goodness and blessings to all people.

In short, the Christian command of integrity is a command to both talk *and* walk in the way of Jesus. It's a life marked by love, compassion, mercy, justice, and honoring God's call above everything else. It's the life spoken of in 1 Peter 3:10-12: *"Whoever would love life and see good days must keep their tongue from evil and their lips from deceitful speech. They must turn from evil and do good; they must seek peace and pursue it. For the eyes of the Lord are on the righteous, and his ears are attentive to their prayer, but the face of the Lord is against those who do evil."* That definition of integrity calls us to walk in the path of Christ and to steer clear of hypocrisy.

I recall a Forbes Magazine article written by Karl Moore and Chatham Sullivan where they discuss what integrity means and why it's so important:

> *"Integrity is that particular quality of character that occurs when a person stays true to their commitments. This means that a person—and in some cases an entire organization—has a point of view about what matters. They declare something of value, and they stick to that endorsement. They do what they say. They stand for something, even if, and especially if they stand to lose something in the process."*

There is no doubt that integrity builds character, which creates the foundation of great leadership. Coach John Wooden said it well: "Be more concerned with your character than your reputation, because your character is what you really are, while your reputation is merely what others think you are." Moore and Sullivan go on to say: "Nothing matters more than integrity at the top. It is the rock foundation for good leadership.

Luke 12: 1-3 NIV states, *"Meanwhile, when a crowd of many thousand had gathered, so that they were trampling on one another, Jesus began to speak first to his disciples, saying, 'Be on your guard against the yeast of the Pharisees, which is hypocrisy. There is nothing concealed that will not be disclosed or hidden that will not be made known. What you have said in the dark will be heard in the daylight, and what you have whispered in the ear in the inner rooms will be proclaimed from the roofs.'"* The parallels between what was said by Moore, Sullivan, and Wooden and what is stated in Luke 12: 1-3 NIV are remarkable but not surprising. Much of today's conventional wisdom is rooted in biblical scripture and teachings but not presented as such. This is unfortunate because it is a missed opportunity to teach God's principles and make an impact on the world. As believers, we must always be aware of these casual classrooms of opportunity to connect Scripture and spread the good news of the gospel!

Your character is who you are at the core of your being. If integrity has no home, you will exemplify what it means to be one way in public but another way in private. People of integrity have no line drawn for their behavior. They are the same whether you are looking at them or not. In this age of social media, anonymity is fast becoming a tool of the enemy to distort and destroy a life of integrity. The ability to shift personalities with the click of a mouse and tap on a keyboard creates an online persona that contradicts the in-person persona. Consequently, relationships in the home, workplace, and most importantly, in the church are eroding

Living with integrity must be premeditated and focused. I learned that I must intentionally disassociate myself from some people, places, and things because they are no longer satisfying or attractive to me. They will not water my spirit and grow me in the way I desire to grow in Christ. They may be part of my world, but they are not who I am. The need to be connected to toxic people, habits, and places erodes the soil, and integrity cannot be planted and flourish in that environment. The ability to be anonymous in sin is intoxicatingly intriguing to someone who is not anchored in the Lord. In my valley on my journey to becoming a woman of GRIT, I had to learn to let go of the false misconception of myself, and I began to exercise these scriptures each day in my daily walk and talk:

> *"Then he said to them all: 'Whoever wants to be my disciple must deny themselves and take up their cross daily and follow me. For whoever wants to save their life will lose it, but whoever loses their life for me will save it.'"* Luke 9: 23-24 (NIV)

> *"Therefore, I urge you, brothers and sisters, in view of God's mercy, to offer your bodies as a living sacrifice, holy and pleasing to God; this is your true and proper worship. Do not conform to the pattern of this world, but be transformed by the renewing of your mind. Then you will be able to test and approve*

what God's will is—his good, pleasing, and perfect will. " Romans 12:1-2 (NIV)

I am sure you have questions about exactly what does it take to be such a person of integrity, flawless in character, peerless in insight, and blameless in scrutiny? Reading through the Bible and rediscovering the story of Daniel, I was able to ascertain his core values. The Bible says that Daniel had an "excellent" spirit within him. Here are some highlights noting his integrity and excellence in leadership, along with my reflections. As you read through the remainder of this section, please note your personal reflections and begin to think about praying for strength in areas of weakness and for strength in areas where you are successful so that you may continue to grow in integrity. My goal with this chapter exercise is that you become aware of how to live a focused and abundant life with integrity as a cornerstone.

1. **Daniel did not conform to world culture** (Daniel 1).
   He was counter-cultural. Without hesitation, he requested that he and his friends be given a different diet than what was on the Babylonian menu. Daniel didn't eat it just because it was put before him. He dared to be different. Daniel was comfortable in his own skin, and he stood out despite multiple efforts to

indoctrinate him in the culture and customs of Babylon. Cultural awareness and engagement are important, but conformity erodes a leader's influence. Romans 12:2 also echoes to us the nonconformist character we must take on to live a life of integrity.

Understanding this, I had to reflect on my life and ask myself the following questions:

- What am I ingesting (eating) from the world that is not food for my soul and nourishment for godly living?

- How am I allowing the culture to define and dictate living a life of integrity? What issues of cultural influence are impacting my integrity?

What is your response to these same questions?

2. **Daniel knew where to go for answers** (Daniel 2:12-18). After the King had a dream that none of the wise men of the kingdom could interpret, a decree was made for all of them to be put to death, including Daniel. But Daniel and his inner circle of trusted companions took the matter to prayer *"to seek mercy from the God of heaven concerning this mystery."* God answered them with the necessary wisdom and

discernment. Daniel was a man of constant communion with God. Prayer was his lifeline; literally... it saved his life on numerous occasions and positioned him for greater influence as a leader.

Through my valley experience and becoming a woman of GRIT, the first area I had to shore up was my prayer life. Remember, I outlined some of the areas that helped me in Chapter 2. It was weak, ritualistic, and inconsistent. I had to conduct an honest assessment and get serious about praying if I wanted to accept God's authority, peace, and favor over my life. Prayer is the thread that sews together my worship and existence.

How would you asses your prayer life?

What are the strengths and weaknesses?

3. **Daniel celebrated wins and praised God for answers when they came** (Daniel 2:19-23). *"Then, the mystery was revealed to Daniel in a vision of the night. Then Daniel blessed the God of heaven... He went on to praise God with a declaration of thanksgiving... To you, O God of my fathers, I give thanks and praise, for you have given me wisdom and might, and* have now made known to me what *we asked of you, for you have made known to us the king's matter."* Daniel knew

where his wisdom came from, and he gave glory and honor where it was due. (James 1:5-8)

So many times, I failed to acknowledge God for how he delivered me or a family member out of a tough situation. I honestly thought I had accomplished it all on my own intellect or lucky break—the excellent illustration of the immature mind of a saved person! Yes, I knew God but did not have a relationship with God. Yes, God had provided me with a great mind bent toward logical reasoning, and that afforded me great wealth and opportunity. However, it was nothing and meant nothing because I was not glorifying God. I am one of those who would roll my eyes at the award shows when someone would open their mouths, and the first words were, "Giving honor to God..." I thought, "you're not in church!" That again, was the immature, saved person speaking. I know I am the church. Thus, I will continually praise God and thank Him for what He has done. It is not my might or power, but His spirit, as Zachariah 4 reminds me.

Do you take time to honor God in every aspect of your life? Do you openly acknowledge before your family, children, coworkers, and neighbors the doors He has opened and miracles He has performed for you?

How are your testimonies and statements received? How does that make you feel? Do you need strength in this area?

4. **Daniel had his friends' back, and therefore could be trusted** (Daniel 2:49). After Daniel interpreted the king's dream, the king paid homage to Daniel, offering Daniel high honors and many great gifts. But Daniel didn't forget his friends Shadrach, Meshach, and Abednego. He made a request to the king that they be appointed over the affairs of the province of Babylon. Daniel understood that at every level of success in life, someone helped you get there. He didn't forget his friends; he remembered those who had helped him. He had their backs!

I made a commitment long ago to continue to open doors for others as they have been opened for me. The favor that God has placed on my life is not to be hoarded but to be shared! My word is my bond; it is integrity at work in a very visible way. I want my friends to know that I say what I mean and mean what I say. I must be deemed trustworthy in every way. Secrets are kept secret, and if I am asked to pray, then I pray!

How have you practiced integrity with your circle of friends?

Do you have a circle where integrity is a bonding agent that has held the friendship together over the years?

What advice are you sharing with younger people about integrity and friendship?

Are you a role model of integrity in this area? What improvements (if any) are needed?

5. **Daniel was willing to lose it all rather than compromise** (Daniel 3). When the king ordered every subject of the kingdom to bow down and worship an idol erected out of Nebuchadnezzar's narcissistic arrogance, Daniel and his three friends counted the cost. They believed their God could deliver them from the fiery furnace. Furthermore, they were still willing to lose everything, including their status, affluence, positions, power, prestige, and even their lives, before they would compromise by worshiping a false god, or self-serving agenda. Their character meant more to them than all the wealth of the kingdom, and they were willing to lose everything before they compromised their character and the God-centered worship that shaped that character.

I am at a point in my life where I must risk losing friends because I have placed God first. Oh, I thought I had God as the head of my life, but I really didn't. In some ways, I took care of everybody and everything before I took care of my relationship with God, and that is so easily manifested in a world that is so stressful with work, family, and friends pulling at you for attention at every tic of the clock's second hand! I had to get my priorities in place. If it had not been for my valley, I would not have grown in this area to become the woman of GRIT I am today. Am I finished growing? No. This is a season of growth. At some point I will be able to rest, refuel, and prepare for the next season of growth and elevation just as the trees do. I must shed people, thoughts, practices, and ideas just as the trees shed leaves. Then, I will be ready for the season of bearing good fruit. Leaves that fell to the ground were composted and turned from negative energy to positive energy once they fell off! Finally, the season of harvest arrives when the fruit is picked and distributed. The fruit adorns me as it clings to me. In order for me to serve my purpose, however, that fruit must be released and used to feed other souls! Oh, what a mighty God I serve who chose to use me in such a way as this! I cannot compromise. If I compromise, I will not grow to my full potential.

Are there any areas where you have compromised God's purpose and plan for your life?

How did that affect you and those around you? What lessons were learned?

Are there any areas that you must re-prioritize? Who can help you? What tools can help you?

6. **Daniel wasn't afraid to have the hard conversation** (Daniel 4:22-27). When Nebuchadnezzar had become enveloped in pride and arrogance, Daniel wasn't intimidated to have the hard conversation about where this conceit was leading the king. He was a straight shooter. He told the king God would drive him into the wilderness to eat grass like a wild beast *"until you know that the Most High rules the kingdom of men and gives it to whom he will."* Daniel didn't pamper the king with flattery; he spoke boldly about the consequences of pride and self-absorption.

Daniel was a straight shooter, but I am sure he allowed his tongue to be led by the spirit. The Bible says that *"Death and life are in the power of the tongue, and those who love it will eat its fruits."* (Proverbs 18:21) Of course, the "tongue" in this verse represents that which tongues produce – words. There are many scriptures that remind us of the power of the tongue including Proverbs 15:1 – *"A soft answer turneth away wrath: but grievous words stir up anger;"* Ephesians 4:29 – *"Let no corrupt communication proceed out of your mouth, but that which is good to the use of edifying, that it may minister grace unto the hearers;"* and Psalm 141:3 – *"Set a watch, O LORD, before my mouth; keep the door of my lips."* Daniel's example is not one that gives us permission just to speak the truth as we see it. Deliberation through prayer with the Holy Spirit in charge of the tongue allowed his words to be received and implemented. I had to learn to pray before speaking as I would go to war with my husband in particular. I wanted so much to get my message across to him to dig into his mind and change his mind, but he seemed to not be able to receive it. I know part of it was the delivery of the message, and the other was he had not prayed either to be able to receive. The power of communication is three-way; it includes you, the Holy Spirit, and God!

In what areas of communication are you needing to adjust style or delivery? How can prayer help you in this area?

7. **Daniel could rightly interpret problems and solve them** (Daniel 5:16). Leaders solve problems; cowards place blame. Leaders find solutions, bosses point fingers. Leaders find a way; whereas, others make excuses. Leaders seek to understand before being understood. They rightly interpret problems and bring about solutions to fix them. The Bible says that Daniel had a gift for solving problems, not blaming others for them.

This really resonated with me since my background in mathematics education and solving problems is a daily occurrence. We have strategies, problem-solving methodologies, formulas, and resources to tap into when it comes to problem-solving. Logical reasoning and organization of thoughts are also required. This is what I do in the workplace. The transfer of this skill to apply in my daily living was relatively successful. I say relatively because I was missing a strategic partner, and that was God. Now that I have incorporated Him and His methods through prayer, I have an arsenal that is well stocked. I had applied my best reasoning to figure out what was wrong in my marriage and apply my best ideas on how to fix it to only be met by a husband who was dead set on walking away. I couldn't fix it. That's when I let go and allowed God to enter into my equation and go to work, and I am trusting Him all the way to the finish line! I needed someone to blame for the chaos. In my marriage, I wanted to make sense out of nonsense. I had to seek to understand. What I sought was God's Word and His divine plan for my life. I prayed for revelation, and that is what happened. I now seek God's direction in other areas. I ask Him to take the skills and intellect He has given me and use it according to His will to achieve the outcome.

How are you handling problematic situations?

What strategies and tools are you using, and how are they working for you?

Do you need to get more God-given strategies in your toolbox for problem-solving?

What areas in your life really challenging?

What specific things do you need God's help with? He's waiting for you to ask Him!

8. **Daniel didn't allow political or cultural influences to erode his values** (Daniel 6). He was a man of prayer and deep faith. This distinguished him above the other political figures of his time, breeding jealousy amongst his colleagues. They set a trap, by passing legislation that would incriminate Daniel for praying to his God, but he paid no attention to it (Daniel 6:10). He never changed his values. He was a man of prayer and unshakable faith regardless of what laws were put on the books or what was culturally acceptable. As a result, Daniel was honored. His leadership and influence increased. The laws were retracted and re-shaped around his values! He didn't bend.

As I studied Daniel 6, I was reminded of a "pre-satellite radio" time when we were in the middle of yet another hurricane in the Houston area. A new talk radio station had just come on the air. I frantically listened nonstop for weather updates for days. In the midst of excellent updates and suggestions for preparation, the station would go back to the talk radio format and take calls. So much of what they talked about were disparaging remarks about groups of people based on country of origin and economic status. As they discussed and as I listened, I found that the more I listened, the more

I was beginning to agree with them, and that was not aligned with what I initially believed. It is true that if you immerse yourself into a culture, you will pick it up. Once I realized this, I had to stop listening to that station. I was being drawn in and allowing negative influences to alter my beliefs. I now immerse myself in sound theology and biblical teachings throughout the day to reinforce the Word of God. I must be knowledgeable enough to know the truth and know when it is being distorted. My influence will never be powerful if I cannot stick with my core beliefs. Of course, there are many who can benefit from a revision of their beliefs, but I have to first get myself together before I can take this show on the road, so to speak!

Honestly, how are culture wars affecting, shaping, or reshaping your values and beliefs?

Are you in a circle of influence that is normalizing bad behavior or modeling integrity and moral standards that can withstand the light of day?

9. **Daniel was a man of integrity; this bred confidence in God** (Daniel 6:22). Charles H. Spurgeon once said, "A good character is the best tombstone." Daniel attributed his great escape from the lion's den to his blameless

character before God. Daniel wasn't perfect by any means. Nonetheless, he understood the correlation of integrity and the providence of God. Psalm 25:21puts it this way: *"May integrity and uprightness preserve me, for I wait for you."* Because Daniel was a man of integrity, he had great confidence in God's deliverance. Daniel boldly personified 1 John 3:21: *"Beloved, if our heart does not condemn us, we have confidence before God."* John W. Gardner wrote, "Men of integrity, by their very existence, rekindle the belief that as a people we can live above the level of moral squalor. We need that belief; a cynical community is a corrupt community."

"If you don't stand for something, you will fall for anything!" is a popular and revelatory quote. Reflecting on the positive correlation of integrity and the providence of God is also affirming to me and energizes me to continue walking my path and seeking integrity at every turn. I must keep using the term "normalizing" as I think about integrity. Our society, some families, and many workplace environments have normalized behavior that in the past was not tolerated at all, and we wonder why the world is so corrupt.

Early in my marriage, my husband frequently recalled stories of coworkers involved in adulterous relationships, and we would sit and discuss the harm of these relationships. Then, the tides turned. He just stopped talking about them, and I assumed all had quieted down. In hindsight, I now see the quiet preceded the storm, and I should have sensed that my marriage was in jeopardy. He stopped talking because he had bitten from that forbidden fruit that was being passed around his workplace like a code of honor. I don't blame them for everything, but they certainly took away accountability filters that would have made it much more difficult to cross the line into adultery.

When the workplace becomes toxic, everyone in that environment is at risk. In my workplace there was a lack of integrity about time, money, and productivity. Laziness and lack were evident. People covered for one another, and the misuse of time was counterproductive. Negative attitudes and beliefs about children and their abilities hindered the success of academic programs.

As I studied this chapter, my mind began to play back decades of stored memories that illustrated what was and was not exemplary of great integrity in the workplace and the community. I am so grateful that I had significant numbers of positive influencers in my life that held me to a higher standard. God was with me every step of the way, and His covering was upon me. Trust me; I am not that strong. I thank God that He always had someone pre-selected to usher me to my next level already in place, which held me accountable in every area of my life.

What examples of "normalization" have you noticed recently that are having negative influences on you, your marriage, your children, your family, your workplace, and/or community?

Have you incorporated these areas into your daily prayer life in order to combat further deterioration?

What examples of great integrity in the workplace and community are you able to point to as models for yourself, your family, and your community?

10. **Daniel trusted God** (Daniel 6:23). *"Then the king was exceedingly glad and commanded that Daniel be taken up out of the den. So, Daniel was taken up out of the den, and no kind of harm was found on him because he had trusted in his God."* Perhaps there's no greater description of this excellent leader. Because he trusted God, he was secure in his own identity.

Because he trusted God, he knew the source of his wisdom. Because he trusted God, he was a man of great, uncompromising courage. Because he trusted God, he lived with integrity and prayed continually. Because he trusted God, he didn't fret his opponents. Daniel never cowered... because he trusted God.

Trusting God at first for me was awkward! I am being honest. You know, I had to trust a God I have never seen with my physical eyes or touched with my hands. Trusting anything unseen or touched just goes against our human nature. As I began to secure an intimate relationship with Him through daily prayer, I learned how to hear Him speak to me. I saw Him manifested in my day, and I could feel His touch because I sought Him! I chased Him! I wanted Him in my life! Trust has to be built on a foundation, and I had to build that foundation with God. He was just waiting for me to come to my senses. I know He allowed this valley experience for me to develop and be prepared for the elevation He already has set aside for me. He has something for me to do in this world, and I must trust Him every step of the way. We face a difficult world each day. I know it is easy to wonder if God even cares. Why do bad things happen? Where is God when I need

Him? In Proverbs 3:12, Solomon reminds us that God never takes a break or leaves us to fend for ourselves *"because the LORD disciplines those he loves, as a father the son he delights in."* Even in the midst of turmoil, God sticks with us and uses challenges to shape us. When we understand that, our perspective completely flips. No longer do we see our setbacks as failures; we see them as moments to glorify God and grow into the life He predestined us to live.

I have learned through my valley that if I'm ever going to trust in God and flee evil, I have to know exactly where I stand. I have to find an objective measure that tells me the truth. And that truth comes from God and His word.

How would you rate your ability to trust God to handle any situation and to bring Him in through prayer?

If you trust God, then you must be willing to release it to Him and not interfere. Are you able to do that?

If so, is there someone you can mentor to get to this place of trust where you find yourself? If not, do you have someone you can go to for mentoring?

In closing, here are a few additional thoughts that summarize Daniel's life of integrity that helped me to focus on how to position myself each day with God:

- Continue to develop my prayer life. I must daily give undivided devotion to God, prayer, and thanksgiving.

- Recommit to a healthy lifestyle. A strong commitment to health and adherence to the Levitical dietary laws will strengthen my body and give me the stamina I need to work for God.

- Acknowledge the value of friendship. I must value, promote, and invest in the welfare of godly friends.

- Live with financial integrity because it is non-negotiable. Daniel wasn't swayed by financial gain. He couldn't be bribed or bought. All money is not good money. I will not sacrifice my Sundays for work unless necessary.

- Grow in faith and courage. I am committed to God until death, with no thought of self-preservation. This is easy to say, especially since we don't face religious persecution in this country. However, the day is coming when Christians will be targeted, and I must be ready.

In what areas of your life are you lacking integrity?

What do you desire out of life that requires integrity?

How has the presence of or lack of integrity impacted your spiritual growth?

What instances and people in your life modeled great integrity or a lack of integrity? How did these models impact your view of integrity?

How has integrity been normalized in your work and home environment? Is the lack of integrity normal?

Do you struggle with "dying to self daily"?

Do you have scriptures that you turn to for help when you are tempted to live out temptations that are contrary to integrity, especially when a lack of integrity has been normalized?

Pray with me now, my beloved reader, for integrity to permeate your soul and become part of your daily walk with our Blessed Savior.

Loving Father, thank You for Christ Jesus, our Lord, Who was the perfect example of a man with a godly character and integrity of spirit. Lord, I long to be more like Jesus in all my thoughts, words, actions, and attitudes today. I pray that You will guard my heart, strengthen my character, and teach me Your ways. I humble myself to Your authority and pray that You will uphold me with

Your righteous right hand. Develop in me the grace and integrity that only comes from being on one accord with Your teachings and intentionally living a life that is grounded in Christ.

Help me today to be true to Your word and righteous in all my doings, and enable me to conquer the temptations, tests, and trials that will inevitably come my way. No weapon formed against me shall prosper today because I submit to You, Lord, for Your protection. I want to live today in a manner that is pleasing to You. Help me to be diligent in my work, faithful in my witness, helpful to those with whom I come in contact, and ready to wait on You for Your right timing and Your best direction.

Give me, I pray, more of Your grace so that I may speak the truth in love. Enable me to grow in sincerity, wisdom, and in the light of Your perfect love. Search out any dark areas of my heart that need to be cut away or pruned back, and circumcise it so that I may be fruitful in Your service, grow in grace, walk in integrity, and be increasingly conformed into the image of the Lord Jesus Christ – in Whose name I pray, Amen.

Living with Integrity

A ny time there is a human relationship, there is an opportunity for integrity or a lack thereof. In its most basic sense, integrity means to live out your life in private in the same way you live (or talk about) your life in public. That's exactly what I am challenged to do as a woman of GRIT!

Christians are called to the highest of ideals. We believe things like "death to self" and "the last shall be first," but we grapple and struggle almost constantly with living lives of integrity. Unfortunately, there are countless examples of Christian leaders who suffered great falls when it was made clear that their private lives looked *vastly* different from the carefully-curated lives they lived in front of their audiences.

Living a Life that Matters

When pressed, I suspect many Christians want to live a life that matters. It's not a bad wish, by any means. These Christians are hoping for a platform to proclaim the gospel in the way they are gifted.

For many people (myself included), a life that matters seems to mean important meetings with important people making important decisions. However, this is not the life to which God calls many of us. To be sure, there are some who *are* called by God to do important things with integrity, but many Christians have mistakenly equated *goodness* with *greatness*. Sometimes that can lead to a life or ministry where someone knows all the right things to say, do, or write to gain a following, but everyday life isn't really impacted.

Let me be clear: If you're in charge of a ministry or a small group, or in any kind of leadership for that matter, but everyone around you thinks you're a jerk, you're not living with integrity. God asks nothing more of us than to live out the fruit of His Spirit. In the words of Philippians 4:8, a life consumed with thinking (and, presumably, acting) on *"whatever is true, whatever is noble, whatever is right, whatever is pure, whatever is lovely, whatever is admirable"* is one of integrity.

Obviously, God can use broken people and broken ministries however he sees fit. People living with no integrity can still be used by God for incredible things—even church leaders who have fallen the farthest and hardest have likely still told someone the truth of God. But that doesn't let us off the hook. God doesn't care how "big" or "small" our lives are, only that we are living lives that are filled with the integrity He commands. It doesn't matter to God if you're a famous person or if the only people who have heard of you are in your community. What matters to God is that you're living with integrity to the commands He has given you. That might mean you become a great leader with a huge following, or it might mean you live a quiet life being the best wife, father, or employee you can be. For me, it meant continuing to honor my marriage vows no matter what it looked like to those looking in. It also meant serving God despite my situation and giving Him my very best, no matter how bad I felt.

How can we live a life of integrity? We must accept God's call to live in His will and walk in the footsteps of Christ. We must live the kind of life that Jesus lived, even if no one is watching us. We must obey the command of James 1:22: *"Do not merely listen to the word, and so deceive yourselves. Do what it says."* It's simple, and it's difficult. And it's all that God asks.

Integrity should be the hallmark of a Christian. The temptation is all around, but God is our rescuer and refuge. We can depend on God to be victorious in this life if we simply trust Him and obey Him. As we strive for trust and obedience, we must be mindful that while so many things are out of our control there is one thing we can control, and that is our character! With God's help, we can behave wisely and make wise decisions.

A person of integrity seeks to follow the Lord's will in everything. Good people don't always win in this life. However, belief in Christ guarantees eternity with God, where we will live in His presence forever. Our integrity does not earn our salvation, but it does bring God's approval. One of the rewards of integrity is pleasing the heart of God. We show our love to God through obedience. Many of us know the truth, but that is not enough—it is time to live it! God demands our loyalty. He seeks people who put Him first above everything and everyone else in their lives. God singled out Job as an ideal example of a man of integrity. The Lord cherishes followers like Job who chooses Him and sticks with Him no matter what. Are you ready to be a "no matter what" type of believer?

Our joy is tied to valuing the instruction of the Lord. The key to integrity is knowing what God expects of us. Ask God to transform your character to that of Christ.

The Bible is the best source of wisdom, for it is God's Word. The closer we live according to Scripture, the more blessings God will grant us, such as the treasure of common sense. Paul taught Titus to lead by setting a good example. Self-control shows spiritual maturity, which manifests God's Spirit in aspects of daily living. A life of humble integrity is above criticism.

We live in a materialistic world where riches can be easily gained dishonestly. Remember that that kind of money or riches is filth in the sight of God. Choose things with eternal value instead. Dishonesty is like spiritual leprosy, eating away at the soul. Children are sponges. They do not learn honesty and integrity from society. Of course, they may be influenced by society, but parents are the first teachers! Children learn from the example of their parents. The Bible confirms this when it says, *"Train up a child in the way he should go; even when he is old, he will not depart from it."* (Proverbs 22:6) People often use this verse as a guarantee that if you raise your children *"in the discipline and instruction of the Lord,"* (Ephesians 6:4) they'll always stay on the right path. That interpretation can be problematic, particularly for the "good parents." I know people who have seen their older children stray from the faith. We all know that we can try our best, and sometimes the results are different from we would have hoped. God has given us free will to make our own choices, after all. However, we have been given our instructions through these scriptures, so we should adhere to them. Be mindful and present each day about what you are teaching your children.

Teach the value of a clear conscience, and that will remain with them always.

Take the Bible to heart. Cling to it. Live by it. Follow its advice and receive the fruit of God's friendship and passionately desire God. Seeking to know and follow him with all of our hearts — in spite of our sinful nature, is the true purpose of life.

The following scriptures provide a broad sampling of passages dealing with the topic of integrity. Select those that resonate with your situation. Make them into prayers, and use them to speak life over your situation. Use the God's word to fight; this is the sword of truth that is used to cut through the enemy and kill his assignment over your life!

2 Samuel 22:26 - To the faithful, you show yourself faithful; to those with integrity, you show integrity.

1 Chronicles 29:17 - I know, my God, that you examine our hearts and rejoice when you find integrity there. You know I have done all this with good motives, and I have watched your people offer their gifts willingly and joyously.

Job 2:3 - Then the Lord asked Satan, "Have you noticed my servant Job? He is the finest man in all the earth. He is blameless—a man of complete integrity. He fears God and stays away from evil. And he has maintained his integrity, even though you urged me to harm him without cause."

Psalm 25:19-21 - See how many enemies I have and how viciously they hate me! Protect me! Rescue my life from them! Do not let me be disgraced, for in you; I take refuge. May integrity and honesty protect me, for I put my hope in you.

Psalm 26:1-4 - Declare me innocent, O Lord, for I have acted with integrity; I have trusted in the Lord without wavering. Put me on trial, Lord, and cross-examine me. Test my motives and my heart. For I am always aware of your unfailing love, and I have lived according to your truth. I do not spend time with liars or go along with hypocrites.

Psalm 26:9-12, NLT - Don't let me suffer the fate of sinners. Don't condemn me along with murderers. Their hands are dirty with evil schemes, and they constantly take bribes. But I am not like that; I live with integrity. So, redeem me and show me mercy. Now I stand on solid ground, and I will publicly praise the Lord.

Psalm 41:11-12 - I know that you are pleased with me, for my enemy does not triumph over me. Because of my integrity, you upheld me and set me in your presence forever.

Acts 13:22 - But God removed Saul and replaced him with David, a man about whom God said, "I have found David, son of Jesse, a man after my own heart. He will do everything I want him to do."

Psalm 101:2 -I will be careful to live a blameless life—when will you come to help me? I will lead a life of integrity in my own home.

Psalm 119:1 - Joyful are people of integrity, who follow the instructions of the LORD.

Proverbs 2:6-8 - For the Lord grants wisdom! From his mouth come knowledge and understanding. He grants a treasure of common sense to the honest. He is a shield to those who walk with integrity. He guards the paths of the just and protects those who are faithful to him.

Proverbs 11:3 - Honesty guides good people; dishonesty destroys treacherous people.

Proverbs 20:7 - The godly walk with integrity; blessed are their children who follow them.

Proverbs 28:6 - Better to be poor and honest than to be dishonest and rich.

Luke 8:15 - And the seeds that fell on the good soil represent honest, good-hearted people who hear God's word, cling to it, and patiently produce a huge harvest.

Titus 2:7-8 - Similarly, encourage the young men to be self-controlled. In everything set them an example by doing what is good. In your teaching show integrity, seriousness, and soundness of speech that cannot be condemned, so that those who oppose you may be ashamed because they have nothing bad to say about us.

CHAPTER 4

Transformation

*All to Jesus, I surrender; all to Him I freely give; I will
ever love and trust Him, in His presence daily live.*

*I surrender all; I surrender all, all to thee, my Blessed
Savior, I surrender all.*

*All to Jesus I surrender; humbly at His feet I bow,
worldly pleasures all forsaken; Take me, Jesus, take
me now.*

*All to Jesus, I surrender; make me, Savior, wholly
thine; fill me with Thy love and power; truly know
that Thou art mine.*

*All to Jesus, I surrender; Lord, I give myself to Thee; fill
me with Thy love and power; let Thy blessing fall on me.*

*All to Jesus, I surrender; now, I feel the sacred flame.
O the joy of full salvation! Glory, glory, to His name!*

J.W. Van Deventer

Glory to Glory

2 Corinthians 3:18 - But we all with unveiled face, beholding and reflecting like a mirror the glory of the Lord, are being transformed into the same image from glory to glory, even as from the Lord Spirit.

As I write, I am continuing to be transformed, remember it is a process. At some point in my immature understanding of the fullness of God, I was naïve enough to think that He would just make everything right if I prayed long enough and loud enough! I mean, I made every attempt in my power to be "good" in His eyes. Therein lied the problem. God's mercy and grace were always sufficient. There was nothing I could do to earn it, and no prayer would ever be long enough or loud enough to put an end to my trial. I realized that this was all predestined and calculated. God leaves nothing to chance, and there are no coincidences.

There is a start and end date already assigned. God molded me on the potter's wheel, and it hurt. I felt every twist and turn, and it hurt. I wanted off the wheel, and I wanted it to be over because it hurt. I prayed to be transformed into that new creature. I prayed Romans 12:2 over myself: *"And do not be fashioned according to this age, but be transformed by the renewing of the mind that you may prove what the will of God is, that which is good and well-pleasing and perfect...,"* and God answered me but not how I wanted Him to answer me. How egotistical of me to have thought for one moment that I had the correct way that God should respond to me. This is the fallacy many of us face; we think we know better than God. Transformation allowed me to accept and honor his authority over my present and my future.

Nonetheless, as you have read, I stayed the course. I dug down deep for strength, and I prayed for God to carry me through. I told Him I would not give up or in. I also told Him I could not do this by myself. I began to realize I was a creature of the environment that raised and nurtured me. I grew up knowing Jesus, knowing scriptures, learning in Bible study and attending church. My life was very nonconsequential. I made good choices a majority of the time. I made good grades, got the education, got the job, and excelled in everything I chose to do. I was selective and didn't chase after everything. I was methodical, analytical, and focused. I was a success in my professional life, and I strived to be a superwoman. Missteps and mistakes happened, but I was resilient and always able to bounce back and actually land with little evidence of interruption—until this time. This time was different, and now I understand why.

God had allowed this to befall me because He was ready to elevate me spiritually. I had acquired the education, technical knowledge, and organizational skills to navigate the corporate world. God waited. God watched. God groomed me through transformation. God transitioned and transformed me through the testing in order to elevate me as a vessel to be used for His glory and kingdom building. I found myself at the crossroad of transformation. This crossroad was the intersection point, the convergence of the manifestation of grace, restoration, and integrity. I knew the transformation was successful (not necessarily complete) when I not only found peace but maintained it.

In this process, I learned that I had erroneously juxtaposed God and my husband. I was looking to God to provide for me the material wealth and success that would be outward signs of successful Christian living. I looked to my husband to give me joy, complete me, and be all I was not—you know, be my other half. This was so out of order. I cannot and will not address what caused my husband to enter into adultery, but I do know that when God has a plan for you that is greatness, a target is immediately painted on your back. I had a target squarely placed on my back, and so did my husband. We chose different ways to engage with the enemy, and we chose different circles to surround ourselves with. I know that my circle empowered me to stand and fight the enemy. My circle drew me closer to God because they all emphasized biblical applications on how to walk through the valley. I believe my husband's circle was one of enablement and mediocrity. Seemingly, a circle that had grown comfortable in dysfunction and had no greater expectation than that of dysfunction had surrounded his life. My transformation allowed the revelation of greatness and rejection of mediocrity. My transformation showed me the imbalance and misplacement. It showed me that I was guilty of idolatry. I had placed more value on my marriage and my husband in an attempt to be the perfect wife. I had devalued my precious God. Nevertheless, His unwavering love for me allowed Him to shower me with grace and mercy.

I continue to pray and stand against the enemy as his assassins still target my marriage. I pray for those who have willingly and unwillingly been co-conspirators in the destruction of this marriage. I thank God for covering me and allowing me to experience His majesty and glory through this valley experience and making me a woman of GRIT.

The Civil War Within

Dr. Martyn Lloyd-Jones, writes in *Spiritual Depression: Its Causes and Its Cures* that "...we must talk to ourselves instead of allowing 'ourselves' to talk to us! ...Have you ever realized that most of your unhappiness in life is because you are listening to yourself instead of talking to yourself? Take those thoughts that come to you the moment you wake up in the morning. You have not originated them, but they start talking to you. They bring back the problems of yesterday. Somebody is talking. Who is talking to you? "Yourself" is talking to you. Once recognized, you must turn on yourself, ...upbraid yourself, ...exhort yourself, and ... remind yourself of God, Who God is, what God has done, and what God has pledged Himself to do. Remind the negative self of the truth that you know, instead of placidly listening to self and allowing it to drag you down and depress you. Does this describe the civil war going on in your mind? A power struggle is going on, and you must tap into the Holy Spirit in order to gain control. Transformation in this area is one I had to battle with day in and day out! It was through prayer and counseling I was able to fight the war and win. Never underestimate the power of a Christian counselor.

Journaling helped me to fight this. I had to become disciplined. I began to jot down some of the things I was rehearsing in my mind each day that were negative barriers to overcoming and achieving the needed transformation of my mind. Energy put into negative thinking was counterproductive and actually zapped my creativity, which adversely affected my ability to be productive.

I had to search the Scripture to find one or two that addressed the specific things I had identified. From there, I began to battle in prayer with the sword of the Spirit. You know it takes the same amount of energy to think positively as it does to think negatively! Put your effort into productive use and developing a relationship with God. This is a perfect example of magnification.

Journaling Activity:

The recurring thoughts I have that cause me discomfort are:

The scriptures I will use to pray against these thoughts are:

My prayer is:

_____

_____

_____

_____

_____

_____

Going Deeper

The word "transformation," according to Merriam-Webster, means "a complete or major change in someone or something's appearance, form, etc." This gives us a basic definition of transformation as a kind of change. But the transformation I experienced has to be looked at through the spiritual eye and not the natural eye.

When we clean up our act, change our behavior to be more Christ-like, or live by a new set of rules and regulations, we may feel that is enough, and we are transformed. Upon deeper inspection of how the Bible deals with the transformation, we find it actually means something different from all of these things.

In the original Greek language of the New Testament, the word used for *transformation* is *metamorphosis*. The biological definition for metamorphosis, again, according to Merriam-Webster, is "a profound change in form from one stage to the next in the life history of an organism, as from the caterpillar to the pupa and from the pupa to the adult butterfly."

Although an outward change in appearance or form takes place, the change comes from within the life of the organism. A caterpillar is born with a life that causes it to become a butterfly. It doesn't put on a butterfly costume or strive to act like a butterfly. As long as it eats, its metabolism takes the nutrients it consumes, assimilates them into the caterpillar, and causes it to grow, so that eventually, the caterpillar changes and becomes a real, genuine butterfly.

A caterpillar changing into a butterfly is an excellent picture of what the Bible speaks of concerning the transformation of the believers into the image of Christ.

Our rebirth with acceptance of Christ as our Savior causes an inner change that transforms us into the image of Christ.

Like the caterpillar, we have to stay in the process of transformation by eating. In John 6:35, Jesus said, *"I am the bread of life; he who comes to me shall by no means hunger, and he who believes into Me shall by no means ever thirst."* Simply put, the Lord wants us to take Him as our daily bread. He is our spiritual food. This is why so many people are empty and looking for people and things to fill the voids that only God can fill. If we want satisfaction—if we desire to be satiated, we must eat Him every day. We eat Him by pouring

His word into our spirit. We eat Him by listening and ingesting His word in music, sermons, and conversations. To transform is to grow and change. We need to eat Him every day in order to fuel the transformation.

Some caterpillars eat only one kind of leaf for their whole lives. In the same way, as believers, we also are meant to eat only one kind of spiritual food throughout our entire lives—Christ. When we eat and drink of Him, we're supplied with His life for our Christian life, and we grow with that life. As we grow, we're in the process mentioned in 2 Corinthians 3:18, "*being transformed from one degree of glory to another,*" little by little, into the image of Christ.

When we consume this steady diet of Christ through conversations, readings, music, and the environment, more of His element is added to us and assimilated by us. We undergo a transformation that's not merely an outward change, but one that comes from our being spiritually nourished and the life of God operating in us.

This is exactly what happened to me. Remember, I did not run from God in this valley experience. I was propelled towards Him because I actively sought Him. I revved up my Bible reading. I accepted the call of ministry on my life once and for all and dove in headfirst. I was drawn closer to Him each day because I made room and time for Him. I felt discomfort when I didn't pray. I became cognizant of His presence. I learned how to listen and hear from God. I have been transformed and now have spiritual eyes and ears and a heart that pumps in rhythm with God's love for me.

I moved into a position of maturity and received God's wisdom to understand what transformation is *not*. I am reminded of Corinthians 13:*11*: *"When I was a child, and I talked like a child, I thought like a child, I reasoned like a child. When I became a man, I put the ways of childhood behind me."* When I was an immature Christian, I thought as a child. Within that childish thinking, I imagined transformation as a change brought about by simply doing good or improving my bad behavior. Genuine change starts within. No amount of makeup can cover up a sinful nature or erase scars that have burdened our souls and held us down with regret and unforgiveness.

My beloved reader, the biggest lesson I learned is that we can't transform ourselves! But we can "be transformed"— that is, we can cooperate with the Lord for this process of transformation to take place in us. To be transformed, we need to take Christ in as our food and our drink each day as we commit to the following:

- sing with our spirit to the Lord

- pray with our spirit

- pray over scriptures

- give thanks to God

- praise God

- preach the gospel or speak about Christ to others

What areas in your life are under attack? Is this a place where you need to submit to God's authority and ask for transformation?

Many of us have been baptized, but are we truly saved? Pray for revelation in your spirit and ask God to transform any areas that are in need of transformation.

My transformation was not one I sought; it came after me. Are you in the same situation? What have you learned about yourself as you have read this book?

Transformation is NOT About Religion; It's About a Relationship

O ne of the residuals of transformation is that God changes our hearts to truly love other people. I found myself convicted to pray for my enemies one morning as I was praying aloud. I was bitter and wanted to blame someone, and there were plenty of people ready to support me in this area of bitterness. But I made a conscious choice that I did not want to reside in the valley of bitterness because it is a barren land. Bitter people are not fun and outgoing. They become very pessimistic and difficult. They love to find other bitter people to connect with. I did not want to become that kind of woman. After all, if that became my countenance, how could I draw to God? Who would want to have what I have if that is what I have as a Christian?

Over the years in so many sermons, I saw how religion pressed the needs of others, the logic of ethical obligation, peer pressure, the fear of bad consequences, etc. In fact, I realized that in many ways, religion exacerbated ill-will and conflict, because, in religion, you get to define your identity self-righteously. In my valley experience, I became self-righteous very quickly. I was quick to condemn my husband, and I wanted the world to know the pain I felt. But that was not going to help me to heal. As a matter of fact, that only cut deeper into the wound, not allowing it to heal. It felt good for only a moment, but then the dark cloud it summoned hung over me for hours, and it was debilitating. I needed to develop my relationship with God in order to be transformed. Yes, I needed the sermons, but I had to balance what I was taking with how God truly calls us to minister to others.

In the process of my transformation, I experienced how God loved me even though I was a sinful mess, and this has helped me to develop compassion, empathy, and humility toward other women going through the same situation—the catalyst that prompted me to write this book. In the process of transformation, I grew in my understanding and appreciation of how deeply sinful I was. At first, I only focused on what my husband had done, how I felt, and the pain I had experienced. I suppose there were times when that reflection was merited. But again, I was magnifying something that would replay in my mind and consume me negatively. I needed to get off that hamster wheel and use that energy to move to a different position. When I used my energy to read the Bible, I became acquainted with how amazing God's love was for all mankind.

That began to transform my mind and my thinking. I began to change what I allowed myself to dwell upon.

Because of the mindset shift, there was a heart shift. My heart began to grow from a selfish position of work to a heart that took joy in sacrificially giving myself away. I became active in the ministry outside my church, teaching classes at a women's shelter for job readiness, going to visit those who I knew were ill, cooking dinner, and delivering them to people in need, cleaning houses for elderly, and any other area where I could help. I put all the excuses aside and happily volunteered. This is the action of a transformed heart. This is what transformation looks like from the inside out. What I learned in this phase of the transformation process was that the more you give God's love away, the more the capacity of your heart is expanded to receive more of God's love!

Reflection

Have you allowed religion to make you justified in self-righteousness? What steps can you take to transform your heart?

Are there areas where you can serve others and grow in the love that reflects how God wants you to transform?

Tapping Into the Root Cause

This is the real work of transformation! I actively sought out a Christian Certified Family Therapist to help me walk through this valley experience. Yes, I prayed, and I had an active life in ministry, but I was also informed enough to know the value of Christian counseling and its ability to unleash God's power to change me in a deep, lasting, and fulfilling way!

Because of counseling, I became aware of two very important principles:

1. Religions sometimes try to combat sinful habits mainly by moral will-power, external restraints, and fear of negative consequences.

2. But at the root of every sinful habit or addiction is a legitimate desire for God's love that you are trying to meet illegitimately— "looking for love in all the wrong places."

So, the ultimate way to overcome every sinful habit/addiction is to learn how to trust in and enjoy God's love.

Remember, I am being transparent with you so that I can help you and myself. I had put my husband on a pedestal, and I thought that all I needed to do was be as perfect as possible—cook great, be a team player, support him and his needs, share my resources, and not weaponized sex. I kept my complaints to a minimum, didn't follow, or look for him when he said he was going out with friends or even away or the weekend. Don't judge me, just listen. I showed him the trust that I knew I deserved. I showed him the love I wanted in return. I was addicted to my husband like a drug because I had put so much effort and energy into creating everything that I thought he appreciated and everything I wanted. I was looking for love that he couldn't give me because he, just like me, was broken. When we actively sought God and prayed daily, we thwarted the enemy. But a crack appeared and was never sealed, and that allowed the division to grow and ultimately destroy the marriage. I ran to God, and he ran in the opposite direction.

I admit I was a shopaholic. I did not consistently overspend our income on clothes and shoes, but when I felt alone or isolated by him, that was how I compensated for the love I needed. Behavior management in terms of setting a budget was not going to get at the root of the problem. The question I had to ask myself so that I could provide an answer in counseling was, "*Why* are you so driven to buy things you don't need?"

My answer: "Because I feel so unattractive and unlovable to my husband that he has left me for someone else." My desire was so strong to be validated and loved that it overrode sound fiscal judgment. Remember, I made good money and was successful, so it was easy for this to become an addiction without much consequence. I was trying to fulfill a core need that God put within me. Unbeknown to me, this was a need that could never be met by any man. I did not know that I was already attractive to the One who made me until I was transformed. He loved me so much, and I was so attractive to Him that he sent Jesus to die so that I may live! Now that is love. And that is the love that transformed me from within so that it no longer matters what I wear or how much I spend. I now rest in the security of His approval of me, and I revel in His delight in me. I have experienced God's undeserved mercy that was used to transform me.

Reflection

Are there addictions that you deal with that are rooted in low self-worth or low self-esteem?

What is your opinion of counseling? Is this something you could benefit from?

The Outward Signs of My Transformation

I tuned in to myself and paid attention to what was happening as a result of allowing God to have His way over my life. I can see the manifestation of my transformation. It is recognizable and tangible. I have lost some friends, but I assure you that I don't dwell on the losses. For every loss, there has been a gain of greater significance. I did experience a temporary period of feeling lost, rejected, and lonely, but once I got through that phase of the transformation, I entered into my current and permanent stage of peace.

1. The traditional rules and beliefs that I grew up with were revisited and reformed. I have replaced religion with an authentic relationship. Traditions and rituals have been replaced with service where my only desire is to glorify God. I have had to learn, unlearn, and relearn so much of the biblical principles and concepts that had been deposited into me. I am now forever intellectually curious about God and the Bible. That curiosity has led me to seek Him. As I have sought Him, I have been cast into a depth of understanding of who He is. This new understanding far surpassed

my own mental capacity to comprehend, and it has truly been supernatural!

2. I accepted the season of suffering and began to see it as a blessing in disguise. I became acutely aware of my negative thoughts and how I reacted emotionally to certain events, people, and circumstances. I learned to block out those triggers and surrendered them to God through daily prayer. In exchange for that surrender, I have received an inner peace that I would otherwise have never known.

3. The focus of my daily energy and talk changed. I used to talk about and do "ordinary" things, and I was perfectly okay with it. My quiet time has increased, and my preference is reading a book or watching an educational documentary that will challenge my thinking and expand my knowledge. I still enjoy my friends and having fun, but it is balanced. I also watch my intake of conversation, and I intentionally avoid gossip. It is negative food for the soul—it depletes rather than supplies!

4. I have an increased desire to learn and discover more about myself. The need to "fit in" with society is not a priority. I am accepting and understanding

Deuteronomy 14:2, *"For thou art a holy people unto the Lord thy God, and the Lord hath chosen thee to be a peculiar people unto himself, above all the nations that are upon the earth"* and 1 Peter 2:9, *"But you are a chosen people, a royal priesthood, a holy nation, God's special possession, that you may declare the praises of him who called you out of darkness into his wonderful light."*

5. My prayer time is important. When I don't get it, I feel off-center. I prefer a quieter time and peaceful environment. I spend a lot of time alone, but I am not lonely. I have become less externally focused on acquisition of material things and outward appearances. Rather, I have begun to experience a deeper exploration of what God wants me to do. At first, I felt like I was overcompensating with prayer. But now, I realize that the silence and solitude I experienced for the past 16 months were necessary for deeper introspection and the quickening of my transformation.

6. On the last day of my 52-day consecration, I leaned in on Luke 2:52 and prayed for direction. As I prayed in the Spirit, out of my mouth came these words: "You are free." I searched my mind and asked for revelation on what that meant. I thought at first, it meant I was

freed from my marriage, and I could get a divorce, but that was not it. Honestly, it was not revealed to me what that meant until this very moment as I write! My freedom was found in my faith! This transformation exposed me to something wonderful that was waiting for me just outside of my comfort zone. I had to be disturbed and my palace of comfort removed in order to receive the gift of freedom. The fear of uncertainty and the unknown outweighed my desire for freedom. But God's plan for transformation proved to be the best plan. I am so glad I surrendered to His will. I am free.

7. I am drawn to beauty in nature and the simple things. I find it difficult to watch some things that I once enjoyed. The violence that has been normalized in many movies and television shows is sometimes unwatchable. I am more guarded about what I consume through my eyes and my ears. I am not a prude, but I am watchful and alert. Everything I ingest has a consequence. The enemy uses small things to distract and influence, but I am now cognizant of his schemes and will not fall for them.

I had often heard and said that "20/20 is perfected in hindsight." Because I have journaled and paid attention to God's whispers, I now fully see that all my suffering and discomfort was a blessing in disguise. I can remember asking God over and over in prayer time, "Why is my life getting worse? Why is my situation not changing? I am being obedient to you; why are you ignoring my prayers? I am making my life better. I am praying, studying, working, fasting, but I don't see a shift. Why Lord have you abandoned me?"

This period of transformation was neither pleasant nor welcomed, but it was necessary. While I was in the midst of it, I often likened it to being held down in water, fighting for breath that was not available. ...Eyes wide open watching the last bubbles of oxygen being released and closing my eyes in acceptance of the imminent end of life. ...Then being yanked out of the water to gasp for air, heaving in as much as possible to compensate for what had been lost. ...Only to repeat, repeat, repeat until I turned this hopeless, helpless situation over to the only One Who had the power to pull me out of the drowning and revive me with the breath of life that was from the beginning the very essence of life by which I was created. I looked at this metamorphosis and realized that some changes were so delicate and complex that they were subtle to the naked eye. Other changes were obvious such as the boldness and confidence with praying for others and standing up to preach and work in ministry.

When this began on July 9, 2018, I had no idea where or how I would land. I prayed that my circumstance would be immediately corrected because God has that kind of power. Silly me—again wanting God to do it my way. As I complete the writing of this book, I am at peace with my marriage, which has not been reconciled. I continue to stand in prayer not for my husband to return to me, but for him to return to God. That deliverance has always been the focus of my prayers for him. I have completely forgiven all the coconspirators who had a hand in the demise of my marriage. I have let go. I have humbled myself to the mighty power of The Creator. I have let God have His way. Only by letting go was I able to undergo the level of transformation required to be at peace, which brought me the power to become a woman of GRIT.

Pray with me now for transformation.

My Heavenly Father, sometimes I can't understand this world I live in and the trials I have endured. I do know that You have made promises to me, and one is to bring beauty from the ashes of my life. You know me better than I know myself, and You know how I have struggled at times to trust You with the broken pieces of my life. You say in your word that without faith it is impossible to please You, and I want to please You more than anything. I want to trust You. I want You to transform me; make me more like Jesus and use my trials for my good and Your glory. Help me believe the promise of Romans 8:28. In the strong name of Jesus I ask, Amen. I thank You for every trial, lessons learned, and yet to be learned. With each trial I am closer to being who and what You desire and designed me to be from conception!

Read over these scriptures, and begin to create prayers for your transformation. Feed on His word so that your soul will be satisfied and will not seek ungodly bread to fill any emptiness you may be experience within.

> *Ezekiel 36:26 - And I will give you a new heart and a new spirit I will put within you. And I will remove the heart of stone from your flesh and give you a heart of flesh.*

> *Romans 12:2 - Do not be conformed to this world, but be transformed by the renewal of your mind, that by testing you may discern what is the will of God, what is good and acceptable and perfect.*

Ezekiel 11:19 - And I will give them one heart, and I will put a new spirit within you, and I will take the stony heart out of their flesh, and will give them a heart of flesh:

Psalm 51:10 - Create in me a clean heart, O God, and renew a steadfast spirit within me.

Romans 12:1-2 - Therefore, I urge you, brothers and sisters, in view of God's mercy, to offer your bodies as a living sacrifice, holy and pleasing to God; this is your true and proper worship. Do not conform to the pattern of this world, but be transformed by the renewing of your mind. Then you will be able to test and approve what God's will is, his good, pleasing and perfect will.

Philippians 1:6 - And I am sure of this that he who began a good work in you will bring it to completion at the day of Jesus Christ.

Luke 6:43-45 - For no good tree bears bad fruit, nor again does a bad tree bear good fruit, for each tree is known by its own fruit. For figs are not gathered from thornbushes, nor are grapes picked from a bramble bush. The good person out of the good treasure of his heart produces good, and the evil person out of his evil treasure produces evil, for out of the abundance of the heart his mouth speaks.

Psalm 139:23-24 - Search me, O God, and know my heart! Try me and know my thoughts! And see if there be any grievous way in me and lead me in the way everlasting!

Jeremiah 32:38-40 - And they shall be my people, and I will be their God. I will give them one heart and one way, that they may fear me forever, for their own good and the good of their children after them. I will make with them an everlasting covenant, that I will not turn away from doing good to them. And I will put the fear of me in their hearts, that they may not turn from me.

My Closing Thoughts

Genesis 1:26-28 - Then God said, "Let us make mankind in our image, in our likeness, so that they may rule over the fish in the sea and the birds in the sky, over the livestock and all the wild animals, and over all the creatures that move along the ground." So, God created mankind in his own image, in the image of God he created them; male and female he created them. God blessed them and said to them, "Be fruitful and increase in number; fill the earth and subdue it. Rule over the fish in the sea and the birds in the sky and over every living creature that moves on the ground."

Sometimes the end doesn't make sense without going back to the beginning. As I reflect on the book of Genesis, it all makes sense to me now. I was transformed in order to fulfill the original mandate in my life. Man was formed in the image of God, but then sin appeared. As a result, you and I were born into sin and had to be delivered from sin through the blood of Jesus. I had to be transformed from my sinful nature and be restored to the original intent of the Creator. The transformation brought out what God had already created inside me. You see, if He breathed life into mankind, that same breath is what creates every life henceforth. It is that same breath stirring my soul and making me yearn to be fed by the Spirit. His bread is what I seek. We each have a longing for God, and it is often misplaced and goes unfulfilled. I had to allow the transformation. Do not be afraid of being born again!

If there is any lesson that I want to leave you with, it is that you are worthy of all the treasures God has already set aside for you on earth and in heaven. Read Genesis 1, and see for yourself. God created the earth and then created man to have dominion and enjoy all the fullness of the earth. You are created by God; therefore, you are powerful—not powerless. You are an heir to His throne. Jesus paid the price, so we could be free to claim our inheritance.

No matter what giant you face, it is your perspective that matters. I magnified the wrong giant when I found myself in my valley. There were two giants that I stood between—my giant God and the giant enemy. I magnified the enemy. I focused on the enemy. I fed the enemy day and night. I gave voice to the enemy. I empowered the enemy. But when I turned and looked at the face of God, everything was put into focus. The enemy was no longer my focus. God became my resting place, my champion. I saw His love and felt His presence.

He carried and cared for me, and I allowed it. He had always been there waiting for me to acknowledge His presence and to welcome Him into my battle. He made me, so He knew what I was capable of. He made you, and you are also capable. My test was a reflection of the strength God had deposited into me, and so is yours. I am giddy with expectations for what the future holds for me, and I trust God with that future. There is hope in my heart and joy in my spirit because I have tapped into the source—I eat the bread of life daily.

This book is a living testament, a labor of true love that reflects the love I have for Christ, and a message of hope for you, the reader. I didn't write it to bash my husband but to release the message of how God has Grace, Restoration, Integrity, and Transformation readily available to you, if you allow Him access into your heart. As I have intentionally sought God's presence in my life and made room for Him, I have grown exponentially in my spiritual life! Notice I did not say "*my religious*" life. Religiosity had actually held me back, making me condescending at times and self-righteous at others. God's grace, these growth experiences, and GRIT overshadowed religiosity to reveal the transparency that is now present in my daily walk with God.

I understand that this trial, this valley experience, was to purge me of all impurities that would hinder my entrance into a higher realm of love, devotion, and service to God. This is also a place where I must dwell a bit longer to see *it* through. The *it* of which I speak is my marriage. I pray daily for others and have begun hosting a prayer line through my church. We have praise reports of answered prayers of healing from cancer, people who have been written off as brain function being diminished to sitting up within hours being fed, and weeks in a coma to miraculously sitting up.

I have to pause here and share this praise report with you. I was about to go to bed the night before my birthday, and I was stirred to pray. So, I did. I began in my bedroom and ended in my family room. The Spirit visited me as I prayed and delivered me a message that someone I had been praying for was being healed at that very moment. Like most times, I was praying aloud. As the words praying to, passionately praising, and joyfully thanking God came of out my mouth, I wept. I turned around in circles repeating my prayer over and over. My heart raced, and I felt pure joy. The next morning, on my birthday, I received a phone call and the message that she was sitting up when her family came to visit!

So many other praise reports have been received, and I look forward to more. But the real take away here is the fact that I have allowed God to transform me into the prayer warrior He always designed me to be. This assignment of prayer is one I take on without hesitation. I have also started a marriage prayer line to pray for marriages and to teach others how to pray for their marriages. Yes, the Bible states that adultery is grounds for divorce. The permission is given to us to divorce, but that is not a command. Through my prayer and supplication over my husband and my marriage, I clearly understand that right now, in this season, I am to stand in prayer and obedience and not turn over my husband to the enemy. I pray for his deliverance each day by using Scripture to cover him. Sometimes the trial we go through is not solely for our benefit but for others to be restored, transformed, and delivered because of our connection and faithfulness to God.

Many days I rest on Proverbs 18:22, which reminds me that *"He who finds a wife finds what is good and receives favor from the LORD."* I am sure you have heard a thousand times that *"God's ways are not our ways,"* and that expression has come alive in my journey. I have yielded all I have to God's will. I finally learned how to turn it over to God, and prayer was the tool I used to turn it over. Transformation was how I was able to achieve peace in this season and maintain love in order to pray from a place of purity, forgiveness, and unconditional love that reflects the Christ in me. Christ is my model of love. Love is a decision we make. Happiness is not a foundation on which to build anything that is lasting. Don't misunderstand me; I am not, nor do I desire to become a martyr for my marriage, but I am a soldier for Christ. Oh, how God has covered me and provided for me is truly amazing. My children are doing extremely well. I have no health issues. I am financially sound. I have time to minister, teach, and volunteer. God has opened the doors to new opportunities, and I readily accept His invitation to walk through them and receive my blessing. I am a woman of GRIT.

My beloved reader, I assure you that I have lost nothing of value. I have gained everything! I have found my truest peace, my resting place, and it is with God. I have been reimagined in my own mind, but first my mind had to be renewed by God so that His wisdom could be deposited into me. I have been released from artificial, self-imposed shackles on my mind that had me bound to a misunderstanding of life. I have gained freedom that was purchased by the blood of the Lamb. I have access to God's unlimited and unmerited grace and mercy. I have been restored and redeemed. I have learned to tame my tongue and speak life over myself instead of condemnation. I have released the anger and hurt to God, and that accelerated my spiritual growth. I have humbled myself to God so that my temper is now ruled by the Spirit. I am now a woman who walks proudly in the path that God had gone before me and prepared. I am not perfect, but I am being perfected bit by bit each day. I am a woman of integrity because I want to please my Holy Father, for I carry His name as a Christian. I have been transformed from within, and it radiates outwardly. I proudly and boldly let my light shine. I desire to be a light that attracts those who are living in ignorance, fear, and darkness. I declare and decree that I serve a living God who is well able to provide my every need. I thank You, Lord, for making me a woman of GRIT!

I pray with you, my beloved reader, one last time.

Our Father, who lives in the heavens above, we honor You and sing Your praises! You are the center of our joy, and there is no other above You. As we encounter the assassins dispatched by the enemy, we trust You to protect and provide for us. We give You all honor and praise to make straight every crooked path. We fight the enemy from a place of power, strength, and victory because the blood of Jesus has been spilled and washed all our sins away. We are no longer in the chains of sins and the wrongdoings of our past! We ask for forgiveness now for all our sins, and the revelation of how we have sinned against you, for our desire is not to live a life that is not pleasing to You. We trusted You, Lord, and lay at Your altar the sacrifice of our lives to be lived from this point forth for Your honor and glory. The idolatry of the past is buried along with every other sin and cast into the sea. We forgive those who have used us, hurt us, abandoned us, and lied to us, and we pray that they will be delivered to You, Lord, and give their lives to You. We thank You for Your grace that is sufficient; we thank You for the restoration of our battle-weary souls and the integrity of Your word that promises us that we will have an abundant life on earth as it is in heaven. We bless Your holy name, bow down to you in humility, and thank you for Your process of transformation. Your transformation allows us to experience You fully and wholly, and it quenches our thirst for You and fills our souls with satisfaction. All praises to You, Lord, Who loves us unconditionally, and we will daily seek You first, and praise You, and run toward You in all areas of our lives for guidance. We lock arms now with You, Lord, and look forward to the day when we see You face to face. We go forth now to spread

Your gospel to all we encounter, and we say thank You, Lord, for all You have done to show us Your unfailing love, in Jesus' name, Amen.

ABOUT THE AUTHOR

Beatrice Moore

Beatrice is a nationally recognized, award winning educator, an international speaker, a minister, entrepreneur, mother, and lifelong teacher. She is a native of San Antonio, Texas. Her professional career path includes a life of service in mathematics education as a secondary mathematics teacher, district supervisor, consultant, and mathematics coach. She has seamlessly integrated her Texas Lifetime Secondary Teacher Certifications in the areas of Mathematics, Spanish, and Journalism into her work with various programs to support improved instruction- with a focus on equity and providing support for under-represented student populations. She has had the honor of working with numerous state and national projects.

During her career, she has been honored with numerous awards including the Benjamin Banneker Association, Inc. 2017 Lifetime Achievement Award; Texas Council of Teachers of

Mathematics Leadership Award, 2015 for exemplary leadership at the state and national level; Governor Rick Perry's Math Initiative Advisory Board, 2002- 2006; TXASCD George H. Brownlee Leadership Award for exemplary leadership in instruction, curriculum and professional development contributions; Houston Business Committee for Educational Excellence Award; Fort Worth/College Board Certificate of Achievement in Academic Excellence; Houston ISD Teacher of the Year Finalist; Recipient of three Houston Business Committee for Educational Excellence grants; and, the Fort Worth Business Alliance Educational Leadership Award.

She has published a variety of professional articles, mathematics textbooks, as well as fiction novels *Shoe Fetish 1* and *Shoe Fetish 2*. To help spread God's promise of abundant life, Beatrice is a contributing author to the anthology, *Journey to Ignite*, a faith-based book which features stories of hope to ignite the soul of the reader.

www.ingramcontent.com/pod-product-compliance
Lightning Source LLC
Chambersburg PA
CBHW071437090426
42737CB00011B/1685